AMISH QUILTMAKER

From Small Projects to Full-Sized Quilts

◆◆◆

Bettina Havig

Sterling Publishing Co., Inc.   New York

To my husband, Alan, who has endured my endless rapture with quiltmaking, my daughter, Kirsten, who asked for an Amish-style quilt to mark her graduation from high school. And to my dear friend, Sara Miller, who helped establish my perspective on the Amish.

Photography for projects 1–29 by Fran Baker.
Edited by Isabel Stein.

Library of Congress Cataloging-in-Publication Data

Havig, Bettina.
    Amish quiltmaker : from small projects to full-sized quilts /
Bettina Havig.
        p.   cm.
    Includes index.
    ISBN 0-8069-8524-0
    1. Patchwork—Patterns. 2. Quilts, Amish. 3. Machine sewing.
I. Title.
TT835.H345   1992
746.46—dc20   92-17121
                                                  CIP

10   9   8   7   6   5   4   3   2

Published by Sterling Publishing Company, Inc.
387 Park Avenue South, New York, N.Y. 10016
© 1992 by Bettina Havig
Distributed in Canada by Sterling Publishing
% Canadian Manda Group, P.O. Box 920, Station U
Toronto, Ontario, Canada M8Z 5P9
Distributed in Great Britain and Europe by Cassell PLC
Villiers House, 41/47 Strand, London WC2N 5JE, England
Distributed in Australia by Capricorn Link Ltd.
P.O. Box 665, Lane Cove, NSW 2066
Manufactured in the United States of America
All rights reserved

Sterling ISBN 0-8069-8524-0

CONTENTS

◆ OVERVIEW OF AMISH QUILTMAKING ◆

◆ PROJECTS ◆

◆ A QUILTING PRIMER ◆

◆ BINDING AND DISPLAYING QUILTS ◆

OVERVIEW OF AMISH QUILTMAKING

HISTORY AND BACKGROUND

The Old Order Amish are a religious sect derived from an Anabaptist group called Mennonites. In 17th-century Europe, disagreement over strict adherences to "shunning," which meant ostracizing nonconforming members, and to other dogma, led to a division around 1694. Those who followed Jacob Amman became known as the Amish. In Alsace–Lorraine, on the border of France and Germany, these strict religious folk were persecuted. They eventually sought and found sanctuary in William Penn's tolerant colony of Pennsylvania, beginning about 1727. Although some Mennonite and Amish immigrants arrived before the American Revolution, most arrived in the United States between 1825 and 1860. Quilting was not among the skills Amish homemakers brought to their new homes; it was introduced to them by their "English" neighbors in the mid-19th century.

The "English" neighbors around their new homes in Pennsylvania were often of Welsh or North Country English roots. The men were accustomed to the hard work of farms and collieries and the women had a rich background of quiltmaking. I believe that it was these associations that introduced quiltmaking to the Amish and Mennonites. Many similarities exist between traditional North Country English and Welsh quilts. The Bars designs we often first associate with the Amish may well have been borrowed from the "strippy" quilts of English tradition. The bonds of friendship formed by women sharing common needs and chores are strong indeed. The Amish retain a German dialect even today, while their neighbors converse in English, as they did earlier; thus, the Amish reference to the "English" is a natural distinction made to sort out friends and neighbors.

The gap in life-styles broadened as the "English" moved into the industrial half of the 19th century and then into the 20th century, replete with automobiles, electricity, airplanes, telephones, and high technology. The Amish strive for self-reliance; they do not want to be tethered to the world. They reject the fancy fittings of a possession-conscious society.

Old Order Amish do not worship in church buildings but in private homes of members. The worshipping body, called a church group, is led by a bishop and preachers. They cling to a simple life-style, rejecting ownership of automobiles and remaining unfettered by power lines and telephones. However, some time-saving devices were readily absorbed into the quiet life-style. The most notable for us is the treadle sewing machine. Since the introduction of the sewing machine to American needlewomen in the mid-19th century, Amish quiltmakers have employed it to construct quilt tops. Traditionally, Amish quilt tops are sewn by treadle machine but are hand-quilted.

Amish communities dot the map in the United States. They thrive and expand, presenting in reality a more fluid culture than one at first imagines. State and local laws providing for educational standards play an important role in locating and maintaining viable communities. German is the primary language of the home. Children add English as a second language at school age. Where the Amish can maintain school standards in combination with German in the home, they can sustain a cloister and retain a greater proportion of young adults. The 1980 census reflected a shift in population concentration; Pennsylvania dropped to second place in Amish population; Ohio was first. Holmes County, Ohio, is now the center that Lancaster County, Pennsylvania, was at one time. Indiana ranks third in Amish population, and Missouri is fourth.

Missouri's Amish population continues to increase, perhaps at a greater rate than that of other states. Communities flourish in several other states. Iowa, Illinois, and Kansas have a long tradition of Amish life. Throughout the upper Midwest, these industrious farm families find new ground to till.

Large families are the norm for the Old Order, as there is much to do and children assume some of the chores and responsibilities incurred in operating a farm with horse-drawn plows and equipment. It takes many hands to milk in the absence of milking machines, and many strong arms and backs to cut and bale, to care for stock, and to cultivate, plant and harvest. Amish girls share in these chores and more. They garden, care for young animals, gather eggs, process and preserve food, and sew. Almost all clothing is made at home, including the bonnets so mandatory for outdoor wear. This sewing generates scraps and remnants for use in quilts.

AMISH DESIGN CHARACTERISTICS

A distinction must be made between *Amish quilts* and *Amish-made quilts*. The latter have no particular relationship to traditional Amish quilts. *Amish-made quilts* are often contracted for: an Amish woman makes the quilt for a fee, which supplements the family income. *Amish quilts*, on the other hand, are made by the Amish for use in their own homes, where restriction to the use of solid-colored fabrics and simple piecing designs distinguish them from the more flamboyant designs that Amish women might stitch for a customer's home.

Conservative Amish quiltmakers always use treadle sewing machines to construct quilt tops and floor frames to stretch the tops for hand quilting. Amish designs are characteristically simple and uncluttered. Compared to the great range of designs used in quiltmaking at large, relatively few pieced designs appear in Amish quilt tops. In general appliqué is not done for use in Amish homes. They consider layering of fabric to be an inefficient use of material. The Amish always act as stewards of their resources.

Solid-colored fabrics are used in quilt tops made for use in Amish homes. Print fabrics are considered to be too worldly for the conservative Amish. In very rare cases, tiny prints may be used for the quilt lining or backing. Even that concession varies depending on the tone of the leadership of the church group or local community.

The projects presented in our book are a sampling of designs of both the early Pennsylvania quilt designs and the Midwestern pieced designs.

Pennsylvania Amish designs are generally bold graphics created by large uncut pieces of fabric such as Amish Bars, Amish Diamond, and Diamond in Square. Midwestern Amish designs are pieced patterns often of the one-patch, four-patch, and nine-patch variety. They are designs utilizing a single predominant template. Baby Blocks, Double Wedding Ring, Ocean Waves, and Sunshine and Shadow are one-patch in concept. These are designs created from a single template used over and over and set together, if necessary, by strips or blocks of fabric. Basic Four-Patch and Nine-Patch, Irish Chains, Shoo-fly, Churn Dash, Bow Tie, and combinations of Nine- and Four-Patch are a few of the straightforward, uncluttered designs used. Strip quilts also meet the needs of these practical quiltmakers. Roman Stripe and Log Cabins, including a variation peculiar to the Amish, allow for complete use of scraps.

Practicality is an important factor in the decisions of the quiltmaker. For the early Amish quiltmakers in Pennsylvania, resources were closer at hand than for their Midwestern cousins. Rather than be completely dependent on scraps, it was not only possible but practical to make quilts of whole cloth or from large sections of fabric. The elimination of tedious cutting and piecing produced tops in much shorter time. Time and energy not spent on piecing was channeled into designing the quilting, thus imparting the rich texture of stitching so admired in Amish quilts. Quilting is essential for the coverlet to be sturdy and serviceable. Unlike pieced work, more elaborate quilting designs did not necessarily mean that more time was needed for the work. For a skilled Amish quiltmaker, marking a quilt to provide for elaborate areas of quilting was not extra work but an extra creative outlet. In the quilting, the superb was separated from the mundane without sacrifice of time. Quilting was a spotlight for the talented needlewoman to demonstrate her skills, so it might as well be the finest quilting design and stitching she could manage. It took no additional fabric or time, and she was expected to do a job using her utmost ability. In short, quilting seems to be a venue where Amish women were allowed to show off.

Where fabrics were more difficult to acquire, quiltmakers relied on scraps and recycled fabric. Midwestern quilts seemed to consume every bit of fabric recovered from garments and household uses. The individual pieces of fabric were smaller but the designs remained simple. One can imagine that scraps were cut to the shape of squares and triangles almost without regard for the final pattern selected. Each time a garment was sewn, the scraps were cut into squares or triangles and put aside for later use. As time allowed, the pieces were assembled into blocks or sections to be set together later.

Characteristically, Amish quilts have borders. Borders are practical. They quickly add size to the pieced top. One border is almost imperative, a second is predictable. The inner border frames and encloses the design. The second, which is usually at least twice as wide as the first, completes the overall design and often provides space for fine quilting. Borders are cut in the most conservative manner. In many instances, borders are interrupted at the side seam and a square is used at the corner. Mitring of corners is rare, as is bias binding. Quilts are bound from the back over or with straight, narrow strips cut to fit each side. No attempt to turn the corner with the same strip is necessary.

Few regional design differences persist today. The Amish are mobile enough that designs have been shared, traditions have been blended, and thus quilts of all types can be found in any single Amish community. What does persist is the simple graphic design, use of solid colors, and fine quilting. The quilts made for Amish homes remain unique and special quilt works.

Contrary to some beliefs, there are no color restrictions imposed on the Amish quiltmaker. Some colors are more prominent, others less so, but all are part of the palette. Lighter colors are obviously harder to keep clean; this practical consideration is the explanation for the scant use of lights and white. There are no restricted uses of any of the colors. The color spectrum presented by young children ambling home from school in the spring or fall would soon dispel any apprehensions about colors. The Amish quiltmaker has always relied on availability. There is little evidence to indicate much use of home-dyed fabrics. No colors are taboo and none are prescribed.

The striking aspect of Amish quilts pivots on the use of color. The juxtaposition of bright and dull hues and the masterful use of light and dark contrast illuminate the quilts. No explanation of what might appear to be a sixth sense for color can be offered. Practice and trial and error will be your companion in these projects. In the book, I make color suggestions, but they are only suggestions, based on experience in viewing and appreciating Amish work and on the advice and counsel of my Amish friends.

You and I cannot make an Amish quilt. We are not Amish. We can admire and imitate their designs and color choices. We can learn from the effective placement of dark and light, somber and gay. We can borrow the simple techniques that make the quilting designs so integral to Amish quilts. However, with all this, we still are not able to duplicate the heritage of Amish quilts. Only one project outlined here is large enough for a bed. It is a consideration to my dear Amish friends not to copy their full-sized bed quilts. The scaled-down size of projects here is, in part, an effort to separate our work from Amish work in the future. The projects given here are generally smaller than quilts produced for Amish homes. It is important not to corrupt the identity of Amish quilts. For this reason I urge you to please sign and identify your work. I fear confusing collectors in the future, since quilts made of solid colors are difficult to document. Signing your works, complete with date and place, will help confirm their origin for future quilt historians.

Amish quiltmaking is as timeless as other factors of their life-style. It is done as it has always been done. The past, the present, and the future are difficult to separate. What I've learned about Amish quiltmaking from my Amish friends is folk history. It was passed to me as it was to them; it is contained in an oral tradition. Unlike "English" quiltmaking, the Amish have no printed history of it, no books of patterns or rules. They don't justify or rationalize the work. They accept it for what it was and is, a necessity of a simple life-style. More than once my questions of "why" were received with a patient expression and the comment, "It is just so." Amish quiltmakers have a wonderful sense of color and harmony, a warm sense of humor, and a balanced perception of their work. They make quilts for all the right reasons. They make them for love—love of the work and love of the people for whom they are intended. With luck, your quiltmaking will take on some of these qualities.

COLOR

Color in Amish quilts is a key factor in the success of the quilt as graphic art, but there are no easy rules. Keep in mind that Amish quilts were traditionally made from the same fabrics used in clothing. The colors selected for an Amish household tend to be dark, cool colors. Given the range of hues and tints, an Amish woman will select for herself dark colors with a tint of blue—blue greens, deep plum, magenta, burgundy, forest green, deep teal, rich chocolate browns, and black. Younger members of the family may have lighter and brighter colors including bright hot pink, sky blue, warm tan, yellow, grass green, and even bright red. Girls' dresses and boys' shirts are constructed by a homemaker in her own home, as are her own dresses and aprons and her husband's shirts. All the outer garments and most undergarments are home sewn.

Contrary to the popular conception, black is not an essential color either for dress or for quilts. Black is the traditional color for some items, such as capes, shawls, and bonnets, but in the range of garments needed it is only a minor color. In the home, decorating colors are sparsely used. Floors are often hard wood with area rugs, woven or braided. Windows are covered with simple curtains and shades. The curtains are selected from a range of sky blue to navy or emerald green to forest green—earth and sky colors. Men's shirts for daily chores are selected from the same range of colors as dresses; however, shirts made for and worn Sundays for church are white. It follows that some white fabric scraps are available, but not in great amounts. There are no religious or cultural dictates to prohibit inclusion of white in quilts. As I researched Amish quilts and their construction, a question I nearly always asked concerned the use of white in quilts. The answer was always the same: white is difficult to keep clean and therefore is used sparingly in quilts.

The daily dress for an Amish woman or girl is a dress and an apron; they rarely are of the same fabric. A dress of sky blue may be topped with a green apron or a lavender dress with a navy apron. The aprons are rotated more often than the dresses as they keep the dresses from getting too soiled and prolong their use between washings.

Typically, a quilt features at least two dominant colors, often three. Designs that are functional for scrap quilts may have pieces that originally were used for garments, gleaned over an extended period of time. The photographs of the examples for these projects provide some suggestions; but remember that these are only *suggestions*. If you select a range of cool, dark colors, try to add a dab of a color that seems out of character. For instance, plan a quilt of slate blue, black, and deep plum; this is a typical grouping, but rather dull. The Amish are not dull. To spark your selections, try a touch of bright aqua or light mauve. The accompanying table (Table 1) gives suggested groups of colors and accents.

Let's not forget white—it is a universal accent, but it too comes in multiple tints. The classic combinations in traditional quilts are also popular with the Amish quiltmaker. Blue, aqua, brown, and red all combine with white in two-color quilts. Remember the admonition about white getting soiled easily, however.

Just a Caution

As you know, there are many shades of any color. Navy, for example, can and does appear in a dozen or more tints. As you collect and select material, you will find some dyes are mixed with more blues while others have more yellow; i.e., some are cool, some warm. Reds range from burgundy to orange, greens range from forest and bottle greens to grass green and pale mint greens. I recommend a color wheel at first to help you place the color in the section of the wheel. A general rule of thumb for the choice of dominant colors is to select from those with greater amounts of blue in the dye and to select accent colors with more yellows or white in the dye. Now that that has been said, be ready to try the surprising and unexpected, not to mention the opposite.

As a first project, I recommend one with only a few colors. It will give you a chance to experiment a little, to see how the colors affect each other, and it will generate scraps for later, more ambitious projects. For scrap quilts, you still need a color that unifies your quilt visually. The Amish choice is generally a cool color such as soft blue, pale green, blue gray, navy, lavender, or black.

For borders, select from colors already included in the central design; the borders also may be constructed of colors not very prominent in the patchwork. Borders may be of fabric newly purchased just for that purpose, or perhaps may be a different dye lot of a color previously used. Unlike our carefully planned recent "English" patchwork, where such a departure might be considered a *faux pas*, Amish quilts may actually be sparked by subtle variation. Recall that Amish quilts usually have two

Table 1. Suggested Color Combinations

Dominant	Accent
Burgundy; royal blue	Olive or avocado
Dark plum; slate blue; black	Bright aqua or light blue or mauve
Deep purple; forest green	Mint green
Turkey red; forest green	Black
Navy; powder blue	Rust or burnt orange
Salmon or coral; tan; camel	Black
Wine; teal	Purple
Wine; teal; purple	Black
Sky blue; purple	Emerald green
Royal blue; gray; black	Bright red
Pink; olive green; mauve	Black
Mint green; purple; forest green; lavender	Black
Teal; bottle green	Hot pink
Deep red (burgundy); purple; black	Powder blue
Slate blue; mauve; deep plum	Black
Burgundy; camel; black	Bright teal
Chambray blue (work-shirt color); brown	Cadet blue
Brown; royal blue	Pink
Deep or royal blue; forest or bottle green	Lime green
Black; lavender; purple	Burgundy
Brown, camel, tan	Turkey red
Teal; purple; aqua	Red
Deep plum; aqua; mauve	Black sateen

borders. To economize, borders may be interrupted at the corners with a separate block. This way it is possible to include four colors in the border of your quilt (inner border, inner squares, outer border, outer squares). You might refer to the chart of color groupings (Table 1) for suggestions. Don't hesitate to construct the pieced section and then take it along with you to your local quilt or fabric shop to try it with various border choices. You will find some unexpected character changes when the colors are laid side by side.

Quilting Designs

The fine quilting on Amish quilts is a hallmark of Amish work. The designs are elegant and elaborately executed, but the techniques for marking are simple—as simple, in many ways, as the quilts themselves. Just as a few piecing designs dominate, a few quilting designs are most popular. Feather designs are prominent. The feathers flow in gracious stems and curves to fill squares, bars and borders. Cable designs are very popular border designs for Amish quilters. Although cables usually appear on borders or strips, they also are used in basket designs.

Careful examination of Amish quilting reveals several other basic motifs that reappear on quilt after quilt. Pumpkin Seed border designs take the name from the four traced pumpkin-seed shapes that form a clover-leaf shape at the center of the squares lining the border.

Fiddlehead quilting motifs appear almost exclusively on Amish quilts. They are a graceful curve reminiscent of fiddlehead fern, but also like a fiddle (violin) neck. Slender leaves fan away from the fiddlehead curve, and the repeated motif lines the wide borders of many Amish quilts. This design occurs on both Pennsylvania and Midwestern Amish quilts.

Very few other life forms appear on Amish quilts. Among them are stylized tulips and roses, possibly acquired from their early Pennsylvania Dutch neighbors. Grape clusters, leaves, and twisting vines appear in abundance. Animal forms such as eagles and doves, which may appear on "English" quilts, are quite rare on Amish quilts.

Templates for marking are cut from any available material and, at first glance, hardly would seem capable of producing the designs we admire. It is with practice that the Amish women produce rich quilting designs from simple tools such as plain cardboard templates.

The quilting designs given in the section on quilting motifs at the back of the book are provided to fit the projects. They are not mandatory. You may select *any* quilting design. No restrictions are placed on Amish quilters; no particular design is prescribed for certain areas.

Patterns and instructions are provided for you to custom design the quilting. No two Amish quilts are identical; no two feathered circles, no two cable borders can be made exact copies of each other. Templates are often used to custom design the quilting as the work progresses. I suggest that you first perfect your design on paper and then transfer it to your quilt top or other project. Specific quilting instructions are not given with each project, so see the section on quilting at the back of the book when you are ready to quilt.

GENERAL INFORMATION

Amish quiltmakers cut templates with the seams included. This is in preparation for treadle machine piecing. A standard seam allowance of ¼″ is used. Borders, large squares, and triangles are measured directly from fabric; no template is used. Projects in this book provide template patterns for most pieced work shown; templates have a seam line and a cutting line for the convenience of those who prefer either method of cutting: (1) marking the template sewing line on the material and then adding ¼″ on all sides to get the cutting line; or (2) marking the template cutting line and lining up the machine sewing foot to sew ¼″ in from the cutting line. For machine piecing, verify your seam allowance to be sure of accurate construction. A very small error can result in a major deviation in final size.

In general, appliqué work is not done for use in Amish homes. Layers of fabric are not considered good stewardship of fabric resources. Solid-colored fabric is used for quilt tops. In very rare cases, very small prints may have been used for the quilt lining or backing.

Borders on Amish quilts are rarely mitred (joined at a 45° angle). Borders are cut in the most conservative manner. In many examples, borders are interrupted at the side seam and a square is used at the corner.

The binding on Amish quilts is most frequently cut from straight lengths of fabric or is formed by having the quilt backing brought over the top for a finished edge. Binding is discussed in detail in the binding section at the back of the book. Specific binding instructions are not given in each project, so consult the binding section after you have pieced the top of your project for that information.

RECOMMENDED TOOLS

The following tools are useful for the projects in this book:

- Several sizes of gridded rulers
- Large cutting mat for use with rotary cutter (this protects table tops)
- Rotary cutter
- Good sharp fabric scissors
- Dressmaker's or other nonpermanent marking pencils suitable for light and dark fabrics
- Yardstick
- Assorted colored threads and wound bobbins
- Good 45° right triangle at least 6″ on each short side
- "Paper" cutting scissors to cut template plastics
- Quilting needles ("betweens," sizes #7 to #10) and quilting thread
- Fine straight pins
- Basting needles—long, fine sharps
- Tracing paper for copying quilting patterns out of the book
- Graph paper and colored pencils, paints, crayons,

or markers for making sketches of possible color combinations
- Thimble
- Masking tape, for marking lines to be quilted and tagging pieces of quilt before it is assembled
- Cardboard or acetate for cutting templates
- Embroidery hoop for quilting small pieces, or larger quilting hoops
- Rectangular quilting frame for holding large projects during the quilting stage. These can be purchased at quilting specialty shops or can be homemade.

WORDS TO THE WISE

- I recommend 100% cotton fabric, broadcloth weight. Prewash all fabrics used. Put them through a regular wash cycle in your washer. This releases excess dyes, preshrinks them, and removes the manufacturer's sizing.
- All yardage given in the book is based on 45″ wide material.
- For machine piecing, press seams as you work (and be grateful if you have an electric iron). Do not steam press.
- All measurements given in this book provide for and include ¼″ seam allowances.
- Patterns for templates also provide for ¼″ seams.
- The choice of bindings is left to your discretion. For some projects a suggestion is made. The two types of bindings most frequently used on Amish quilts are detailed in the section on binding at the back of the book. Yardages for backings generally provide enough for either choice.
- Color suggestions, when included in project directions, are based on colors found in antique or vintage Amish quilts or on colors used in the models given in this book.
- Background quilting (quilting to fill background areas and give emphasis to motifs) is recommended for use behind any feathered designs.
- Batting dimensions given are generally 2″ larger on each side than the expected size of the top.

(They are trimmed after quilting.) Batting is usually sold prepackaged.
- Always check the size of the inner panels and inner borders before cutting fabric for the next border. Small variances in seam allowances can cause finished sizes to vary.
- Save all your solid-colored scraps!
- *Always* complete the quilting before binding or finishing the edges.
- Generally, borders are added to the sides of the quilt and then to the top and bottom. An inside border is completed before another border is added.
- When ⅛ yard is suggested (remember, all yardage is based on 45″ wide material), you may have an equivalent piece such as 12″ × 17″, 10″ × 20″, 9″ × 22″ that will be enough.
- The Amish sometimes quilt with black thread—but not always! They may select any color thread; often it will be selected to match the back of the quilt so that a bed quilt may be used with the back up as a whole-cloth design. You may even use white and off-white threads.
- Backings (or linings) for Old Order Amish quilts are also of solid-colored fabric. Mennonite quilts often use small prints. If you are not Amish, you might consider using prints, plaids, or stripes.
- Amish quiltmakers, especially in the first half of the 20th century, often used lightweight wool challis for quilts. It's lovely to work with but good solid-colored wool challis is expensive and sometimes difficult to find. Please consider its use in a special project.
- Cotton batting was the most frequent choice until the advent of polyester batting. Now polyester batting is preferred because it is fairly easy to quilt and requires less quilting to stabilize it.
- Sizes of right triangles are given by the length of the two short sides (legs) when templates for triangle pieces are not given in the book.
- Construction in projects is done with right sides of material facing each other unless otherwise noted. Diagrams show the right side of the fabric unless otherwise noted.

1. Amish Diamond in Square Quilt, Variation I

24″ × 24″ (61 cm × 61 cm)

Traditionally, the Amish Diamond in Square design is identified as typical of the Pennsylvania Amish. It is a bold design, possibly copied from leather-covered prayer books. Each piece is to be measured and cut without a template. This truly emulates the construction procedure used in an Amish quiltmaker's home.

The bold graphics allow for very lovely quilting designs. A feathered circle in the center square is graceful and flowing, and by filling the background properly with straight-line designs the feather designs are enriched and enhanced. (See "Quilting Motifs" at the back of the book, Figure Q16.)

All measurements include ¼″ seam allowance. After cutting a triangle, trim the acute points back ⅜″ to eliminate excess fabric—cut at a right angle to the longest side of triangle (Figure 1–1).

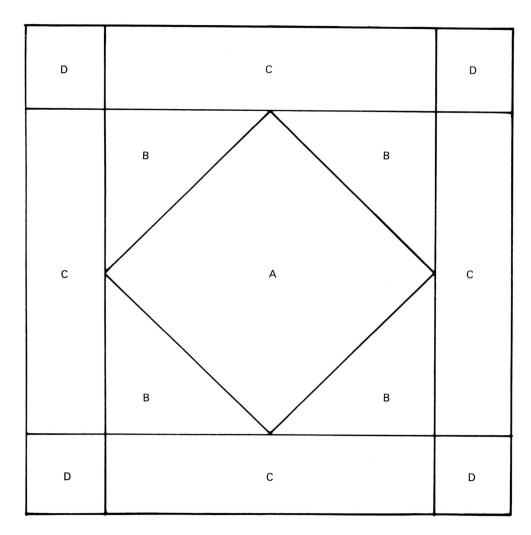

Diagram of finished Amish Diamond in Square, Variation 1.

YARDAGE

PIECE	COLOR*	AMOUNT
A	1	⅜ yard
B	2	⅜ yard
C	3	⅜ yard
D	4*	¼ yard
Backing	Your choice	⅞ yard
Batting	—	28″ × 28″

* If color for D is repeated from colors 1 or 2, no additional yardage is required.

CUTTING FOR VARIATION I

PIECE	COLOR	QUANTITY	SIZE
A	1	1	11¾″ × 11¾″
B	2	4	8⅞″ × 8⅞″ right triangles*
C	3	4	4½″ × 16½″
D	4	4	4½″ × 4½″

* That is, the short sides of the triangles are each 8⅞″.

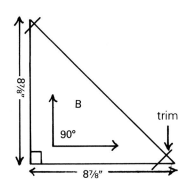

1–1 *Diagram of Piece B. Arrows indicate straight grain of fabric.*

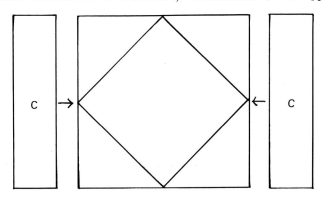

1–3 *Stitch strips (C) to opposite sides of center panel.*

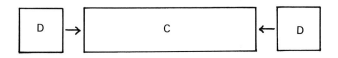

1–4 *Join corner pieces (D) to short ends of each remaining strip C.*

CONSTRUCTION

All construction in the project is done with seam allowances of ¼".

1. Stitch triangles B to each side of square A (Figure 1–2). After attaching each triangle, flip it out of the way, cut the thread, and start a new line of stitching to attach the next triangle.
2. Stitch a strip C to two opposite sides of the center panel (Figure 1–3).
3. Join corner pieces (D) to each short end of the remaining two C strips to make the final border units (Figure 1–4).
4. Join the border units to the top and bottom of the center panel (Figure 1–5). This completes the quilt top. Press the quilt top.
5. See quilting and binding instructions at the back of the book to finish the project.

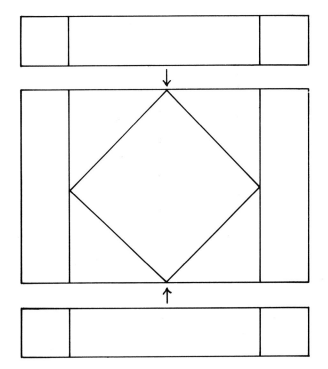

1–5 *Join border units to the top and bottom of the center panel.*

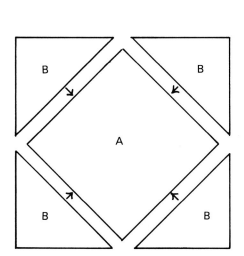

1–2 *Stitch triangles (B) to each side of Square A.*

2. Amish Diamond in Square Quilt, Variation II

36″ × 36″ (91.4 cm × 91.4 cm)

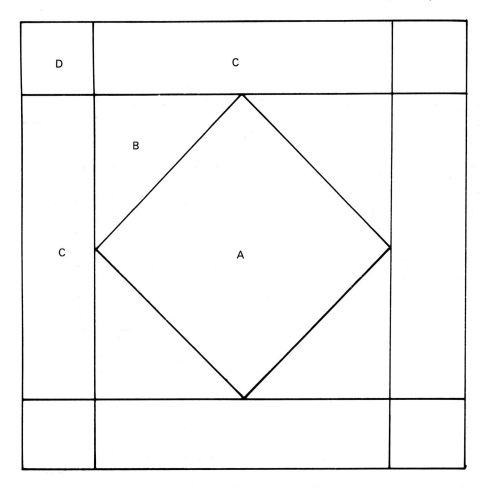

Diagram of finished Amish Diamond in Square, Variation II.

YARDAGE FOR VARIATION II

PIECE	COLOR	AMOUNT
A	1	½ yard
B	2	⅜ yard
C	3	¾ yard
D	4*	¼ yard
Backing	—	1⅛ yard (trim to 40″ × 40″)
Batting	—	40″ × 40″

* If color for D is repeated from Colors 1 or 2, no additional yardage is required.

CUTTING FOR VARIATION II

PIECE	COLOR	QUANTITY	SIZE
A	1	1	17½″ × 17½″
B	2	4	12⅞″ × 12⅞″ right triangles*
C	3	4	24½″ × 6½″
D	4	4	6½″ × 6½″

* The short sides of the right triangles are each 12⅞″.

CONSTRUCTION

1. Follow construction order for Variation I, consulting diagrams there.
2. Press the completed quilt top.
3. See quilting and binding instructions at the back of the book to finish the project.

3. Diamond in Square Quilt, Double Border (Variation III)

40″ × 40″ (101.5 cm × 101.5 cm)

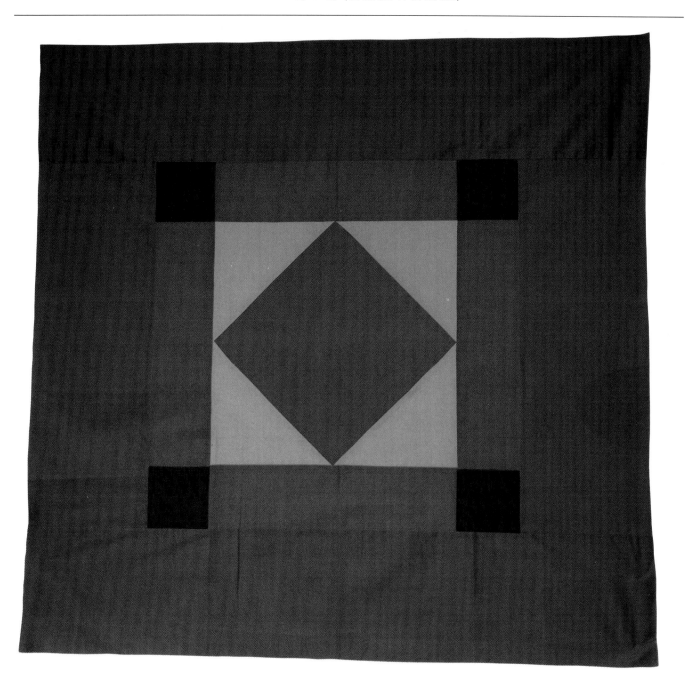

Variation III uses the Amish Diamond in Square (Variation I) as the center and adds borders to increase the finished size to 40″ × 40″.

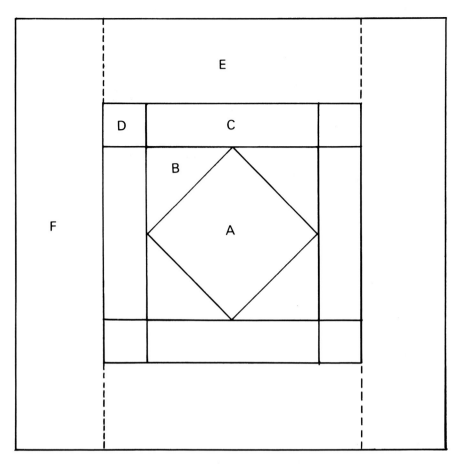

Diagram of finished Amish Diamond in Square, Variation III.

YARDAGE FOR VARIATION III

PIECE	COLOR	AMOUNT
A	1	⅜ yard
B	2	⅜ yard
C	3	⅜ yard
D	4	¼ yard
E	1 or 2	1 yard
F	1 or 2	1 yard
Backing	—	1¼ yards
Batting	—	1¼ yards (trim to 44″ × 44″)

CONSTRUCTION

1. Follow construction for Variation I, consulting diagrams there.
2. Attach short border strips (E) to top and bottom of central design (which is completed Variation I).
3. Add long border strips (F) to each side of the central design.
4. Press the finished quilt top.
5. See quilting and binding instructions at the back of the book to finish the project.

CUTTING FOR VARIATION III

PIECE	COLOR	QUANTITY	SIZE
A	1	1	11¾″ × 11¾″
B	2	4	8⅞″ × 8⅞″ right triangles*
C	3	4	4½″ × 16½″
D	4	4	4½″ × 4½″
E	5	2	24½″ × 8½″
F	5	2	40½″ × 8½″

* Short sides of triangles are each 8⅞″.

4. Double Diamond in Square Quilt (Variation IV)

48″ × 48″ (121.9 cm × 121.9 cm)

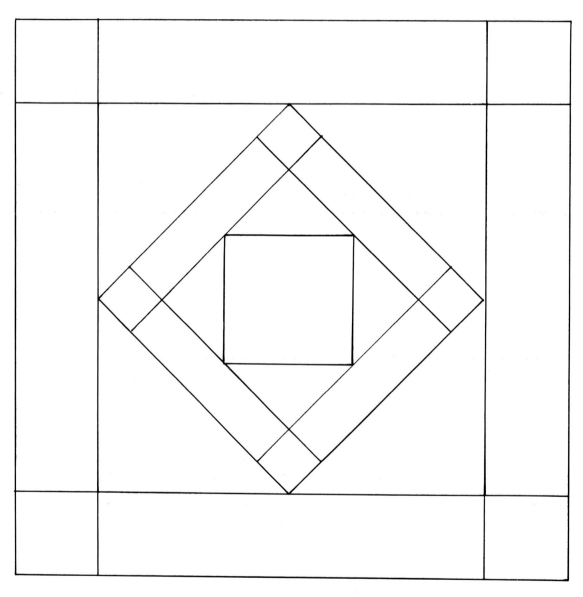

Diagram of finished Double Diamond in Square.

The Double Diamond in Square project uses the Amish Diamond in Square (Variation I) as its center. The colors of the outer pieces may repeat some of the inner design colors.

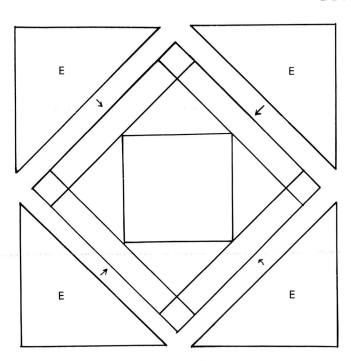

4–1 *Attaching the E triangles in the Double Diamond in Square.*

CONSTRUCTION

1. Construct Variation I, which is the center of the Double Diamond in Square. See diagrams with Variation I (Project 1) for the order of piecing.
2. Attach the E triangles to the four sides of the Variation I unit you made in Step 1 (Figure 4–1).
3. Press all the seams toward the outside.
4. Sew an F strip to the two opposite sides of the main design, as shown in Figure 4–2.
5. Join the corner squares (G) to each short end of the remaining two borders (F).
6. Sew the G–F–G border unit to the top and bottom edges of the pieced panel, matching seams.
7. Press the finished quilt top.
8. See the quilting and binding instructions at the back of the book to finish the project.

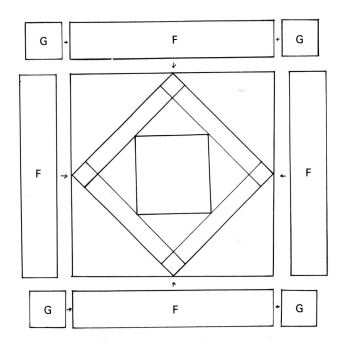

4–2 *Attaching the F strips in the Double Diamond in Square.*

YARDAGE FOR VARIATION IV

PIECE	COLOR	AMOUNT
A	1	⅜ yard
B	2	⅜ yard
C	3	⅜ yard
D	4	¼ yard
E	1, 2, 3, or 4	⅝ yard
F	1, 2, 3, or 4	1 yard
G	1, 2, 3, or 4	¼ yard
Backing	—	2¼ yards (pieced to 52″ × 52″)
Batting	—	52″ × 52″

CUTTING FOR VARIATION IV

PIECE	COLOR	QUANTITY	SIZE
A	1	1	11¾″ × 11¾″
B	2	4	8⅞″ × 8⅞″ right triangles*
C	3	4	4½″ × 16½″
D	4	4	4½″ × 4½″
E	1, 2, 3, or 4	4	17⅞″ × 17⅞″ right triangles*
F	1, 2, 3, or 4	4	34½″ × 7½″
G	1, 2, 3, or 4	4	7½″ × 7½″

* Dimensions given are short sides of right triangles.

Double Diamond in Square Quilt (Variation IV).

5. Square in Diamond in Square Quilt
(Variation V)

40″ × 40″ (101.6 cm × 101.6 cm)

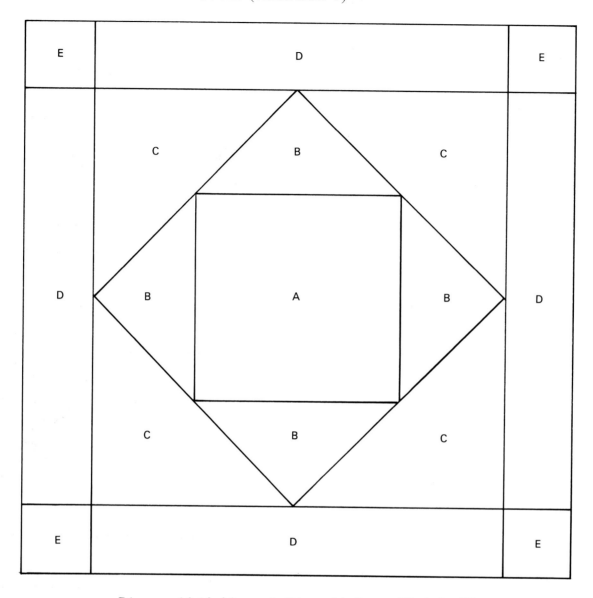

Diagram of finished Square in Diamond in Square (Variation V).

YARDAGE

PIECE	COLOR	AMOUNT
A	1	⅜ yard
B	2	⅜ yard
C	3	½ yard
D	4	¾ yard
E	5*	¼ yard
Backing	Your choice	1¼ yards
Batting	—	44″ × 44″

* If E is repeated from any previously used color, no additional fabric is required.

CUTTING

PIECE	COLOR	QUANTITY	SIZE
A	1	1	15½″ × 15½″
B	2	4	11½″ × 11½″ right triangles*
C	3	4	15⅞″ × 15⅞″ right triangles*
D	4	4	30½″ × 5½″
E	5	4	5½″ × 5½″

* Dimensions given are short sides of right triangles.

CONSTRUCTION

1. Sew B triangles to the sides of square A (Figure 5–1). Press the seams on the sides formed by the B pieces to the outside edges.
2. Sew C triangles to the sides of the pieced panel created in Step 1 (Figure 5–2). Press the seams outward.
3. Add two borders (D) to two opposite sides of the pieced panel created in Step 2 (Figure 5–3).
4. Sew corner squares E to the short ends of each of the two remaining D strips (Figure 5–3).
5. Sew the border strip units E–D–E created in Step 4 to the top and bottom of the pieced panel made in Step 3, matching seams.
6. Press the finished quilt top.
7. See quilting and binding instructions at the back of the book to finish the project.

The five variations of the Amish Square given in projects 1 through 5 represent just a few of the possibilities. Remember that you can repeat colors or use a subtle variation of a color to add interest.

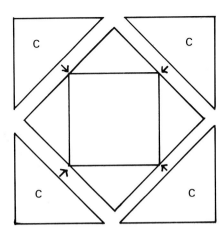

5–2 *Attaching inner triangles to central pieced panel, Square in Diamond in Square.*

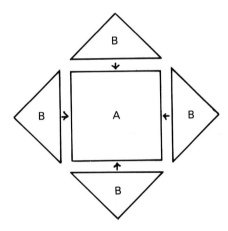

5–1 *Attaching triangles to central square A for Square in Diamond in Square.*

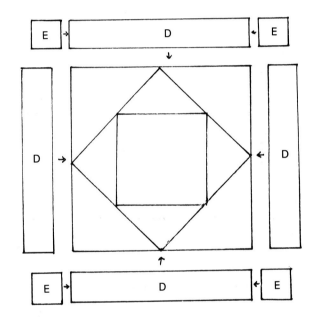

5–3 *Attaching border units, Square in Diamond in Square.*

6. Amish Bars Quilt, Variation I

24½" × 24½" (62.2 cm × 62.2 cm)

The Amish Bars design is attributed to the Pennsylvania Amish of Lancaster County; however, it may have its roots in English quiltmaking tradition. The construction is very simple and the bars allow for a variety of quilting motifs. No templates are provided for the bars—we are still working in the Amish tradition, so the measurements are given for you to cut the pieces.

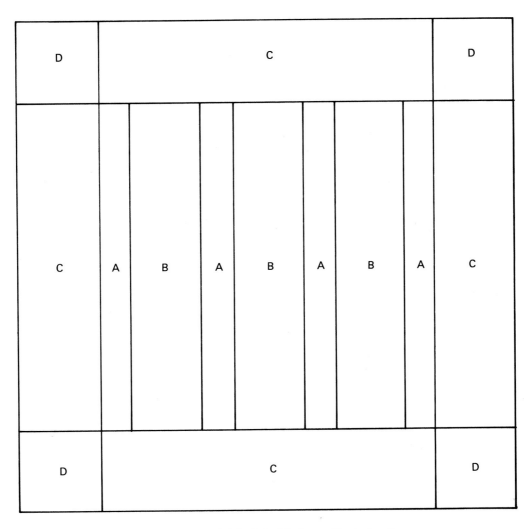

Diagram of finished Amish Bars, Variation I.

YARDAGE

PIECE	COLOR	AMOUNT
A	1	¼ yard
B	2	¼ yard
C	3	¼ yard
D	4*	¼ yard
Backing	Your choice	¾ yard
Batting	—	27″ × 27″

* D may be made with Color 2 from scraps of B instead.

CUTTING

PIECE	COLOR	QUANTITY	SIZE
A	1	4	2″ × 17″
B	2	3	4″ × 17″
C	3	4	4½″ × 17″
D	4	4	4½″ × 4½″

CONSTRUCTION

1. Piece the center panel (A's and B's) as shown in Figure 6–1.
2. Sew two border pieces (C) to opposite sides of the center panel you made in Step 1, attaching them to A strips, as shown in Figure 6–2.
3. Sew corners D to each of the two remaining C borders at the short ends. This order of piecing allows for seam adjustments, if necessary, to the length of the top and bottom C borders.
4. Attach border units D–C–D created in Step 3 to the top and bottom of the unit created in Step 2 (Figure 6–2).
5. Press the finished quilt top.
6. See quilting and binding instructions at the back of the book to finish the project.

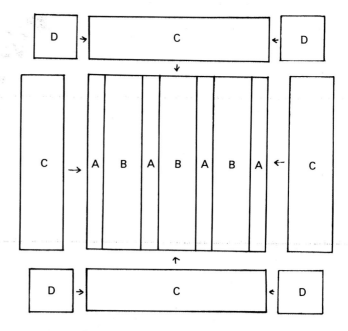

6–2 *Piecing borders and corners, Amish Bars, Variation I.*

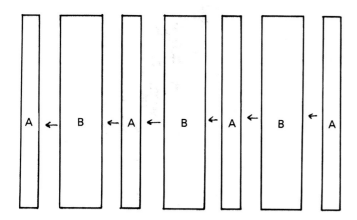

6–1 *Piecing stripes in Amish Bars, Variation I.*

7. Amish Bars Quilt, Double Border (Variation II)

84″ × 104″ (213.4 cm × 264.2 cm)

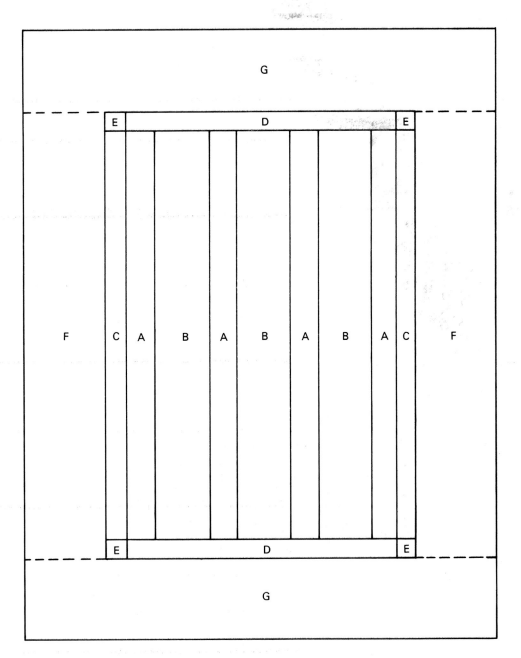

Diagram of finished Amish Bars, Variation II.

Amish Bars, Variation II.

YARDAGE

PIECE	COLOR	AMOUNT
A	1	1⅞ yards
B, E	2	1⅞ yards
C and D	3	1⅞ yards
F and G	4	4½ yards
Backing	Your choice	9 yards
Batting	—	90" × 108"

CUTTING

PIECE	COLOR	QUANTITY	SIZE
A	1	4	5" × 63½"
B	2	3	9½" × 63½"
C	3	2	5" × 63½"
D	3	2	4" × 45½"
E	2	4	5" × 5"
F	4	2	14½" × 72½"
G	4	2	14½" × 82½"

CONSTRUCTION

1. Beginning with Strip A, alternate strips A and B; sew them together as shown in Figure 7–1 to form the center panel of the design.
2. Sew the long inner border strips (C) to each side of the center panel created in Step 1, as shown in Figure 7–2.
3. Join corners E to each short end of the short inner border strips D; see Figure 7–2.
4. Sew the E–D–E border unit created in Step 3 to the top and bottom of the central panel created in Step 2 (Figure 7–2).
5. Stitch F side outer border strips to either side of the unit created in Step 4, Figure 7–3.
6. Stitch G (top and bottom outer border strips) to the top and bottom of the unit created in Step 5.
7. Press the finished quilt top.
8. See quilting and binding instructions at the back of the book to finish the project.

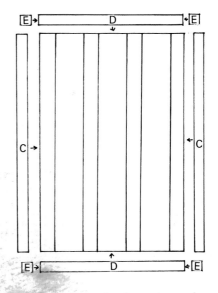

7–2 *Attaching inner border strips and corners, Amish Bars, Variation II.*

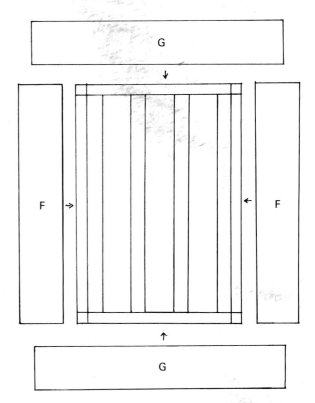

7–3 *Attaching outer border strips, Amish Bars, Variation II.*

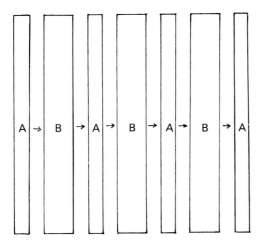

7–1 *Piecing diagram for bars, Amish Bars, Variation II.*

8. Double Irish Chain Quilt

25½″ × 25½″ (64.8 cm × 64.8 cm)*

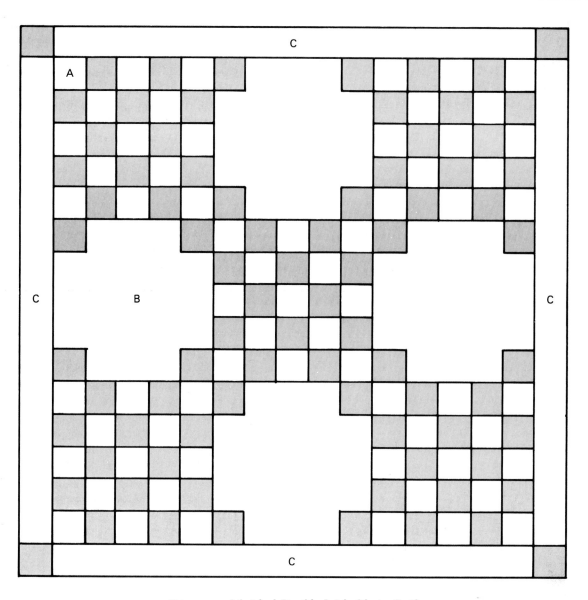

Diagram of finished Double Irish Chain Quilt.

Irish chains, especially Double Irish Chains, are very popular Amish designs. The construction is simple and very uncluttered, and a nice open area allows for a pretty quilting motif. The traditional construction method includes appliqué. In this case it produces the most efficient use of time, even though appliqué is rare in Amish quiltmaking.

---

* Final size if optional outer border is used will be 33½″ × 33½″ (85 cm × 85 cm).

Double Irish Chain Quilt.

YARDAGE

PIECE	COLOR	AMOUNT
A, B, and C (inner border)	1	¾ yard
A	2	⅜ yard
Outer border (optional)*	Your choice	⅝ yard
Backing	Your choice	⅞ yard
Batting	—	28″ × 28″

* Not shown in photo or diagrams.

CUTTING

PIECE	COLOR	QUANTITY	SIZE
A	1	65	2″ × 2″
A	2	80*	2″ × 2″
B	1	4	8″ × 8″
C	1	4	2″ × 23″
Outer border strips (optional)	Your choice	4	4½″ × 26″
Outer border squares (optional)	1 or 2	4	4½″ × 4½″

* Four are reserved for borders.

CONSTRUCTION

1. *Overview:* There are two basic units or blocks to be pieced. Unit I (Figure 8–5) is composed of 25 squares in a checkerboard pattern. Unit II is an alternate block with a small square appliquéd (i.e., sewn on top of the big block) at each corner. You will construct 5 of Unit I (Figure 8–5) and 4 of Unit II (Figure 8–6).

2. *Chain piecing.* What often takes so much time when piecing small units by machine is starting and stopping and cutting threads. Chain piecing eliminates a few steps by avoiding cutting threads at the end of each seam. For your Double Irish Chain, sew two small squares (A), one each of colors 1 and 2, together and, without stopping to cut the threads, slip another pair of squares under your needle (see Figure 8–1). Continue until you have completed 60 pairs. There will be just a couple of stitch lengths of thread between pairs. Cut the threads to separate the stitched pairs.

3. Now you have 60 pairs like those in Figure 8–2 and you're ready to connect the pairs to make a rectangle or strip of four squares as shown in Figure 8–3. Press the seams of each strip toward the darker colors. You can chain piece these strips of four squares. You will need 30 strips of four squares to make all the Unit I blocks.

4. You have 5 lonely "A" squares of Color 1 left when you complete the strips of four squares. Take a strip of four squares and attach a Color 1 "A" square to the Color 2 end of it as shown at the bottom of Figure 8–4. Repeat this 4 more times to make five units of five squares. Each goes across the bottom of the checkerboard pattern in Unit I when it is assembled.

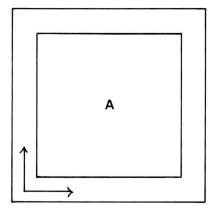

Full-size template A for Double Irish Chain. Outer line, cutting line. Inner line, seam line. Arrows indicate straight grain of fabric.

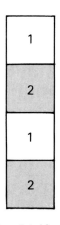

8–3 A strip of 4 blocks for Unit I in the Double Irish Chain Quilt.

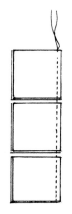

8–1 Chain piecing (right sides of material are together).

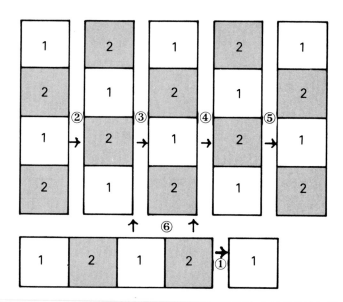

8–4 Order and positioning of strips of 4 squares to form one Unit I in the Double Irish Chain Quilt. Circled numbers indicate order of piecing.

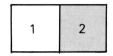

8–2 A pair of "A" blocks for the Double Irish Chain Quilt. Numbers indicate colors.

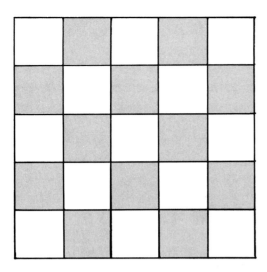

8–5   Diagram of Unit I, Double Irish Chain Quilt.

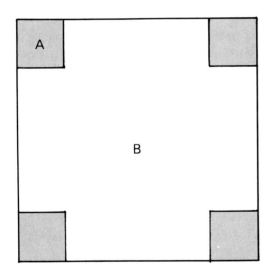

8–6   Diagram of Unit II, Double Irish Chain Quilt.

5. To make Unit I, assemble 5 strips of four squares and the one strip of five squares, following the positioning of the strips given in Figure 8–4. The circled numbers indicate the order of construction. Seam the five strips of four squares together vertically as shown. Then add a strip of five squares across the bottom to complete the Unit I checkerboard (Figure 8–5).

6. Repeat Step 5 four more times until you have made 5 checkerboard Unit I's.

7. *Constructing Unit II* (*Figure 8–6*): Appliqué four small "A" squares of Color 2 to the corners of each 8" B square. Start by turning under two sides of the two small squares ¼" and pressing them. Position each "A" square so that the cut (unfolded) edges of the small square are on top of the cut edges of the corners of square B. Appliqué "A" onto B using a blind stitch and colored thread matching Color 2.

8. Repeat Step 7 until you have made 4 Unit II's (see diagram of finished quilt).

9. Arrange units I and II as shown in Figure 8–7 and stitch them together, first joining them in rows and then completing the design by joining the rows together.

10. Attach two border strips C to two opposite sides of the central pieced panel that includes all the Units I and II, which you created in Step 9. Sew an A square of Color 2 to the short end of the remaining two C borders to make an A–C–A unit.

11. Attach the A–C–A border units to the top and bottom of the central pieced panel you made in Step 10. This completes the Double Irish Chain quilt top. Press the quilt top.

12. See the quilting and binding instructions at the back of the book to finish the project.

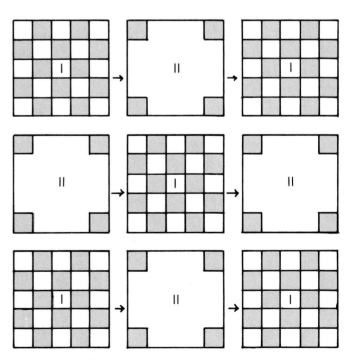

8–7   Order of joining Units I and II for Double Irish Chain Quilt.

9.　Sawtooth Bars Quilt

28″ × 38″ (71.1 cm × 96.5 cm)

This pattern was shared with the author by Mrs. Jake E. Gingerich, who made a similar quilt. Her quilt (which was much larger) was made for a double bed and her pattern was taken from an older quilt that had long since worn out. The "pumpkin seed" border quilting motif for the inner border acquired its name from actual pumpkin seeds, used as templates for the quilting design.

The seeds are nestled in echoed squares and they are very popular to fill narrow borders, usually the first (inner) border on a double-bordered quilt. The "fiddlehead" design used in the outer border is unique to Amish quilts. We believe it takes its name from the fiddlehead fern. Most life forms incorporated in the quilting designs of Amish quilts represent plants rather than animals and are of the mundane "garden" variety. Often the actual plant leaf becomes the model or template.

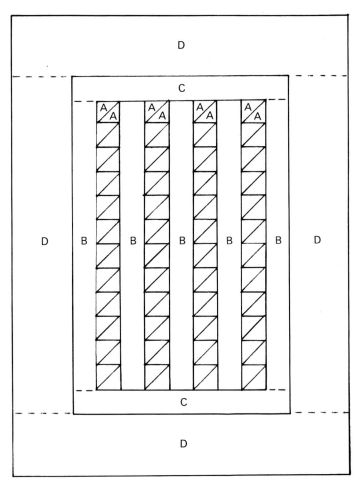

Diagram of finished Amish Sawtooth Bars.

YARDAGE		
PIECE	COLOR	AMOUNT
A	8 to 12 varying colors	⅛ yard of each color, or scraps totaling 1 to 1½ yards
B and C	1	½ yard
D	2	¾ yard, cut on crosswise grain (from selvage to selvage)
Backing	Your choice	1 yard
Batting	—	32″ × 42″

CUTTING			
PIECE	COLOR	QUANTITY	SIZE
A	Varying	96	Template A
B	1	5	2½″ × 24½″
C	1	2	2½″ × 18½″
D	2	4	5½″ × 28½″

CONSTRUCTION

1. Sew 4 sawtooth bars by taking 24 triangles of size A and constructing 12 squares, each square of which is made of 2 A's (Figure 9–1a). (Do not use two identical color triangles together in a square.) When joining the triangles in pairs, you may chain piece to save time (Figure 9–1b). Join the squares into sawtooth strips (Figure 9–1c).

2. Beginning with a plain bar (B), sew a plain bar (B) to a sawtooth bar, followed by a plain bar (B), followed by a sawtooth bar, and so on, ending with a last plain bar (B) (Figure 9–2). Press the entire unit.

3. Sew border strips (C) to the top and bottom edges of the bar unit created in Step 2 (Figure 9–3). Press.

4. Sew two outer border strips (D) to the opposite sides of the unit created in Step 3 (Figure 9–3).

5. Sew the remaining two outer border strips (D) to the top and bottom of the unit created in Step 4 (Figure (9–3).

6. Press the finished quilt top.

7. See quilting and binding instructions at the back of the book to complete the project.

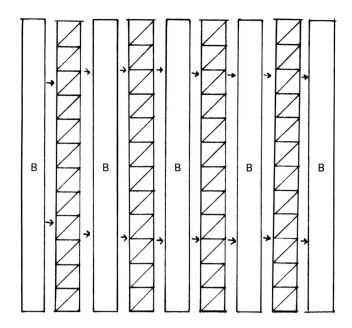

9–2 *Piecing order for attaching plain and sawtooth bars.*

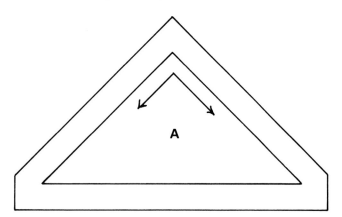

Template A, for piecing sawtooth bars (full size). Outside line is cutting line. Inside line is seam line. Arrows indicate straight grain of fabric.

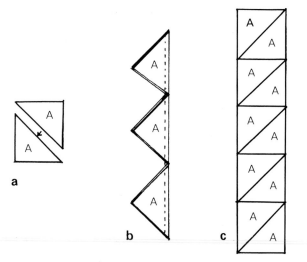

9–1 *Piecing diagrams for making sawtooth bars: (a) joining two triangles; (b) chain piecing; (c) make pieced strips twelve squares in length for each sawtooth bar.*

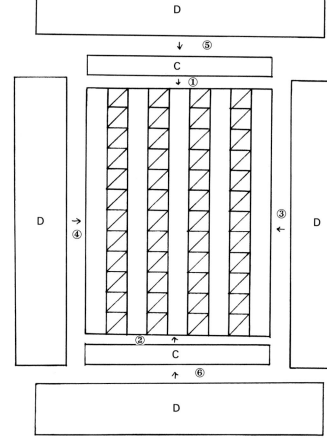

9–3 *Order of piecing borders for Sawtooth Bars.*

10. Basic Pillow, Diamond in Square

12″ × 12″ (30.5 cm × 30.5 cm)

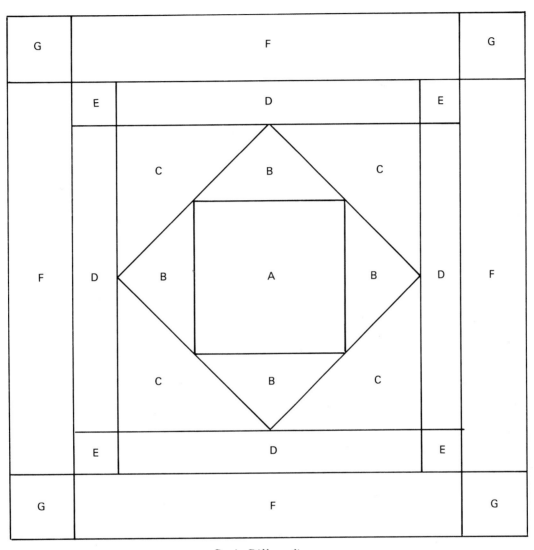

Basic Pillow diagram.

The basic pillow is a scaled-down layout of a classic Amish quilt, consisting of a center pieced panel, an inner border with corner squares, and an outer border with corner squares. Most furniture in Amish homes is constructed with straight lines and rarely is overstuffed. Pillows like the ones in this book might be used on rockers, chairs, and dining benches. They are great small projects and wonderful ways to experiment with color. A series of these pillows used as a color study will stretch your appreciation for color and color interaction. If you already have enough pillows, you can frame these projects as you would a print and arrange them in a cluster. Remember to allow an air spacer in the frame, to extend the life of the block.

I hope you'll have fun with the pillow variations given in projects 10 through 21. They all grow from one basic design with different center variations. In Project 10 we give the basic layout for the pillow construction. In projects 11 through 21, patterns for variations of the center panel are provided, including full-size template patterns where needed. The pillow patterns represent a small collection of block designs popular with Amish quiltmakers. Because of the small scale of the center designs, you may prefer hand piecing them, rather than machine sewing them. Most of the pillows have a double border. You simply substitute center designs, as indicated. The variations fit within the outer borders, All pillows are 12″ × 12″ finished size. Select your variation, and piece and construct your pillow top. Center panel patterns provided are: Basic Diamond in Square; Churn Dash; Ohio Star; Fruit Basket; Single Wedding Ring; Evening Star; Eight-Point Star; Star of Bethlehem; Bow Tie; Double Nine Patch; Bear's Paw; and Whole Cloth designs.

All of the quilting designs to be done in the pieced centers follow the seam lines and are set in ¼″ from the seams. Cable designs span the double or single borders. Full-size quilting motifs for the borders are given in the quilt motifs section at the back of the book. None of the pillows suggests the use of a ruffle (not very Amish—too fancy).

Color placement numbers are used only when they augment the development of the design. If none are indicated, be adventurous and see what evolves. You may wish to refer to the color suggestion chart presented in the "Color" section at the beginning of the book.

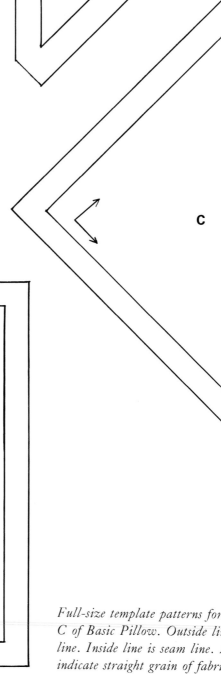

Full-size template patterns for A, B, and C of Basic Pillow. Outside line is cutting line. Inside line is seam line. Arrows indicate straight grain of fabric.

Basic Pillow, Diamond in Square.

YARDAGE, BASIC DIAMOND IN SQUARE

PIECE	COLOR	AMOUNT
A	1	⅛ yard
B	2	⅛ yard
C	3	⅛ yard
D	1 or 2	⅛ yard
E	1, 2, or 3	1½″ × 6″
F	1, 2, or 3	⅛ yard
G	1, 2, or 3	2″ × 8″
Pillow back	1, 2, or 3	⅜ yard
Batting	—	16″ × 16″
Muslin or batiste	—	16″ × 16″

CUTTING, BASIC DIAMOND IN SQUARE

PIECE	COLOR	QUANTITY	SIZE
A	1	1	Template A
B	2	4	Template B
C	3	4	Template C
D	1, 2, or 3	4	1½″ × 7½″
E	1, 2, or 3	4	1½″ × 1½″
F	1, 2, or 3	4	2″ × 9½″
G	1, 2, or 3	4	2″ × 2″
Pillow back	1, 2, or 3	1	12½″ × 12½″
Batting	—	1	12½″ × 12½″
Muslin or batiste	—	1	12½″ × 12½″

CONSTRUCTION

1. Stitch B triangles to central square A, as indicated in Figure 10–1. Press seams toward outside.
2. Stitch C triangles to center pieced panel you created in Step 1 (Figure 10–2).
3. Attach two side inner borders (D) to opposite sides of the center unit created in Step 2. Stitch E squares to both short ends of the remaining two inner borders (D) (Figure 10–3). Press seams.
4. Stitch E–D–E inner border units to top and bottom of the center unit created in Step 3 (Figure 10–3).
5. Attach two side outer border strips (F) to opposite sides of the unit created in Step 4 (Figure 10–4).
6. Stitch G squares to both short ends of the remaining two outer border strips F (Figure 10–4). Press seams.
7. Stitch G–F–G outer border units to the center unit created in Step 5.
8. Press your pillow top.
9. See quilting instructions at the back of the book and Completing and Stuffing a Pillow, below, to finish the project.

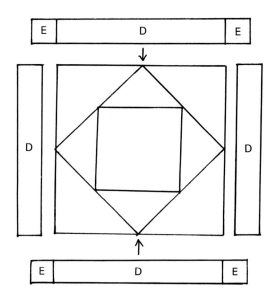

10–3 Attaching inner borders to Basic Pillow.

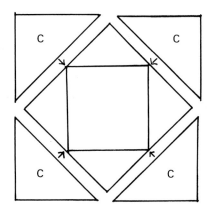

10–1 Attaching B triangles to central square, Basic Pillow.

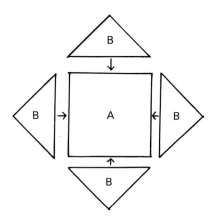

10–2 Attaching C triangles to central unit, Basic Pillow.

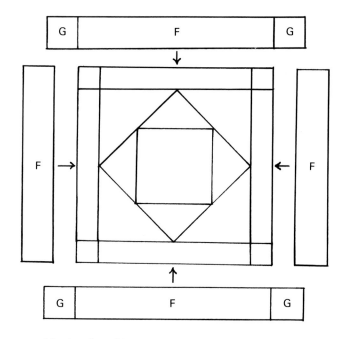

10–4 Attaching outer borders to Basic Pillow.

COMPLETING AND STUFFING A PILLOW

1. Cut your pillow top backing, muslin, and batting 2" larger in each dimension than your pillow top's unfinished size (so make them 14½" × 14½"). Hand baste the pillow top, batting, and muslin together. You are making a sandwich with the pillow top facing out, the batting in the middle and the muslin facing out on the bottom. Your basting will hold the three layers flat and snug while you quilt. I prefer basting first in a spider-web manner, always working from the central area to the outer edge, and then I superimpose a further rectangular grid of basting (Figure 10–5). The "spider

web'' eases the excess fullness out. The grid reinforces the positioning. Finally, run a line of basting completely around the edge of the pillow (or quilt) top about ⅛"–¼" from the outer edge. Do not remove the basting around the edge, even after the quilting is complete. It will help control the edge while you complete the pillow.

2. Transfer your quilting pattern and proceed with the quilting. (See the quilting section at the back of the book.)

3. The Amish way to complete your pillow uses the simplest possible construction. It involves no placket or zipper—never a zipper. Cut a square of fabric for the outside back of your pillow that is 12½" × 12½"; use one of the fabrics you chose for the top design. If you want to give the backing body, cut a square of batting 12½" × 12½", and also cut a square of muslin or batiste 12½" × 12½". Make a textile "sandwich" of the three layers: backing–batting–muslin, and hand baste through all three layers to hold them together. Otherwise you can simply use the backing by itself.

4. Place the pillow top face-down against the outside of the pillow back unit (back–batting–muslin or just backing, whichever you chose). Pin the pillow top to the backing unit along the outer edges of all four sides. To attach the pillow top to the backing unit, begin stitching on the bottom edge of the pillow about 2" in from a corner (remember that the seam allowances are all ¼"). Proceed with stitching the first side until you are ¾" from the upcoming corner. Then turn the fabric to make your sewing line at an angle as you sew across the corner to the next side (see Figure 10–6). The angled corners will help control and soften the sharp points at the pillow corners. Continue stitching to within 6" or 8" of the place where you started to sew, turning the corners in the manner just described. Then stop stitching and backstitch for one inch (1") to end the seam. You have left a 6" to 8" opening in the pillow so that you can stuff it.

5. Trim off the excess material at the corners of the pillow unit to within ½" of the seam line so that it may be turned easily without bunching up at the corners.

6. Gently push the entire pillow top and back unit through the 6" to 8" opening you left so that the entire pillow cover is now turned right-side out.

7. Stuff the pillow until it is moderately firm. The stuffing will compact with use, so don't understuff.

8. Turn in the edges of the pillow opening and whipstitch them to each other with matching thread.

Note: If you wish, you may use a 12" pillow form instead of stuffing, but it's not the Amish way. The Amish often use pillows as chair seat cushions. If you wish to use them in this manner, you may use less stuffing.

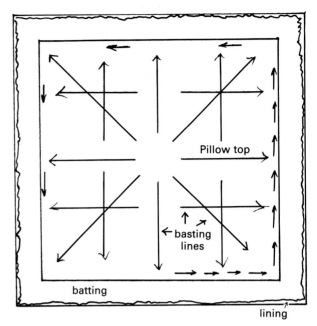

10–5 Basting diagram for pillow top (any pillow).

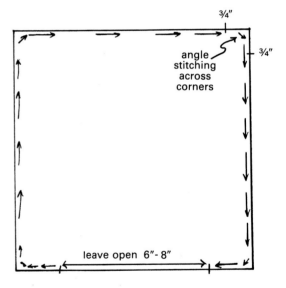

10–6 Sewing line for attaching pillow top to back unit. Arrows indicate stitch lines (there are ¼" seam allowances).

11. Churn Dash Pillow

12″ × 12″ (30.5 cm × 30.5 cm)

The Churn Dash design, based on a 9-patch central square, is one of the oldest and most popular simple patchwork designs.

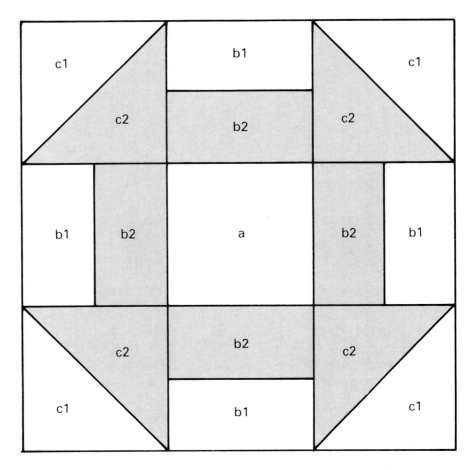

*Diagram of completed Churn Dash block (3½″ × 3½″),
which replaces Piece A in Basic Pillow. Numbers indicate
colors.*

The Churn Dash block given here will be 3½″ × 3½″
when finished and can be substituted for Piece A in the
Basic Pillow (Project 10).

CUTTING

PIECE	COLOR	QUANTITY	SIZE
a	1	1	Template a
b1	1	4	Template b
c1	1	4	Template c
b2	2	4	Template b
c2	2	4	Template c
B	3	4	Template B*
C	2	4	Template C*
D	4	4	1½″ × 7½″
E	1	4	1½″ × 1½″
F	3	4	2″ × 9½″
G	2	4	2″ × 2″

YARDAGE

PIECE	COLOR	AMOUNT
a, b1, c1, E	1 (Pale gray)	⅛ yard
b2, c2, C, G	2 (Dark gray)	⅛ yard
B, F	3 (Pinkish orange)	⅛ yard
D	4 (Black)	⅛ yard
Pillow back	Choose one of above	⅜ yard
Batting	—	16″ × 16″
Muslin or batiste	—	16″ × 16″

* Colors in parentheses are colors in model.

* Use Template B and C from Basic Pillow Project 10.

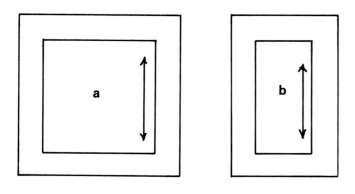

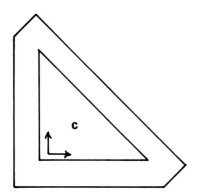

Full-size template patterns for Churn Dash block. Inside line is seam line. Outside line is cutting line. Arrows indicate straight grain of fabric.

CONSTRUCTION

1. Take four c triangles of Color 1 (we will call these triangles c1) and four triangles of Color 2 (c2). Sew them together to make four squares; each is made of one triangle c1 and one triangle c2 (see Figure 11–1, corners). Chain piecing (see Figure 9–1b) will save time and thread.

2. Take four b rectangles of Color 1 (b1) and four rectangles of Color 2 (b2). Assemble them in four squares, each having a b1 and b2 rectangle (see Figure 11–1, middle of top). You can chain piece them also.

3. Press the squares created in steps 1 and 2.

4. To complete the 9-patch grid for the Churn Dash block, sew the squares together in 3 columns, as shown in Figure **11-1**. Be sure to turn the squares in the correct direction to make the pattern. Then sew the columns together to complete the block.

5. The Churn Dash block replaces Piece A in the Basic Pillow. For the rest of the Churn Dash pillow top construction, follow the construction steps given in Project 10, starting with Step 1.

6. To complete the pillow, see instructions in Project 10 on "Completing and Stuffing a Pillow."

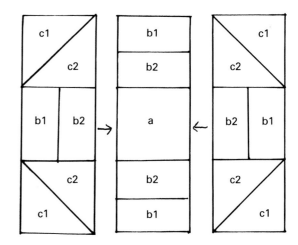

11–2 Assemble the squares in 3 columns; be sure to turn them correctly to make the Churn Dash design. Then assemble the columns to make the block.

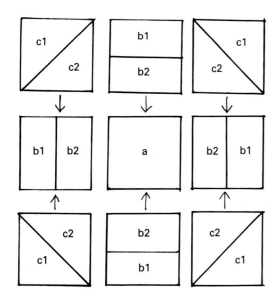

11–1 The 8 assembled squares around the "a" center of the Churn Dash block.

12. Ohio Star Pillow

12″ × 12″ (30.5 cm × 30.5 cm)

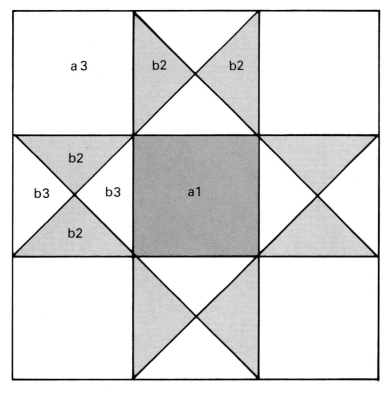

Diagram of finished Ohio Star.

It is fitting for Ohio, which currently has the largest population of Amish, to be represented by a block design. The Ohio Star block replaces Piece A in the Basic Pillow (Project 10). Select three colors for the Ohio Star design. The yardage given is enough for the rest of the Basic Pillow top as well; you can decide which colors to use for each part.

YARDAGE

PIECE	COLOR	AMOUNT
a1, B, E, F	1 (Red in model)	⅛ yard
b2, D, G	2 (Black in model)	⅛ yard
b3, a3, C	3 (Light orange in model)	⅛ yard
Pillow back	Your choice	⅜ yard
Batting	—	16″ × 16″
Muslin or batiste	—	16″ × 16″

CUTTING

PIECE	COLOR	QUANTITY	SIZE
a	1	1	Template a
b	2	8	Template b
b	3	8	Template b
a	3	4	Template a
B	1	4	Template B*
C	3	4	Template C*
D	2	4	1½″ × 7½″
E	1	4	1½″ × 1½″
F	1	4	2″ × 9½″
G	2	4	2″ × 2″

* Use Templates B and C from Basic Pillow, Project 10.

Ohio Star Pillow.

CONSTRUCTION

1. With right sides of material together, create eight pairs of triangles (b) by attaching them on one short side (Fig. 12–1). Each pair has one triangle of Color 2 and one of Color 3. Chain piecing may be used (see Project 8). Note that the long triangle sides aren't attached to anything in this step.

2. Construct 4 pieced square units out of the triangles you created in Step 1, being sure to follow Figure 12–2 for correct positioning of the colors.

3. Take the 5 squares of size "a" (four of Color 3 and one of Color 1) and attach them to the squares you created in Step 2, following Figure 12–2 for positioning and making three columns of 3 squares each.

4. Sew the columns of squares together to complete the Ohio Star construction (Figure 12–3). Press the block.

5. The Ohio Star substitutes for Piece A in the Basic Pillow (Project 10). For the rest of the Ohio Star pillow top construction, follow the construction steps given in Project 10, starting with Step 1.

6. To complete the pillow, see instructions in Project 10 on "Completing and Stuffing a Pillow."

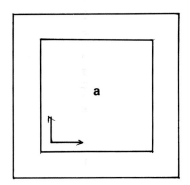

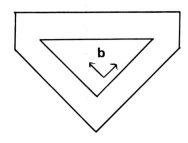

Full-size templates for Ohio Star. Outer line is cutting line. Inside line is seam line. Arrows indicate straight grain of fabric.

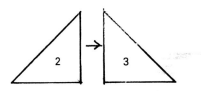

12–1 Attach pairs of triangles on short sides. Numbers indicate colors.

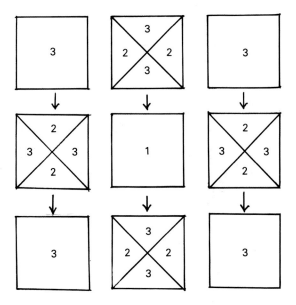

12–2 Guide for attaching squares, Ohio Star. Numbers indicate colors.

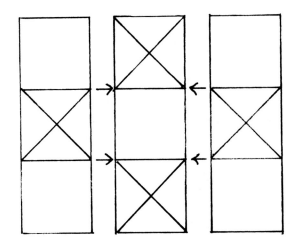

12–3 Attach groups of squares together, matching seams.

13. Fruit Basket Pillow

12″ × 12″ (30.5 cm × 30.5 cm)

A number of pieced basket motifs appear in Amish quilts. The Fruit Basket used here is shown in three colors.

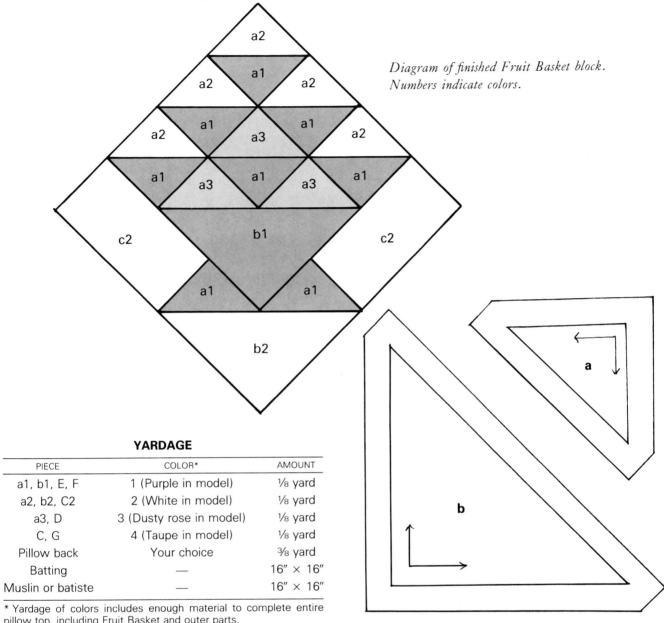

Diagram of finished Fruit Basket block. Numbers indicate colors.

YARDAGE

PIECE	COLOR*	AMOUNT
a1, b1, E, F	1 (Purple in model)	⅛ yard
a2, b2, C2	2 (White in model)	⅛ yard
a3, D	3 (Dusty rose in model)	⅛ yard
C, G	4 (Taupe in model)	⅛ yard
Pillow back	Your choice	⅜ yard
Batting	—	16″ × 16″
Muslin or batiste	—	16″ × 16″

* Yardage of colors includes enough material to complete entire pillow top, including Fruit Basket and outer parts.

CUTTING

PIECE	COLOR	QUANTITY	SIZE
a1	1	8	Template a
a2	2	5	Template a
a3	3	3	Template a
b1	1	1	Template b
b2	2	1	Template b
c2	2	2	Template c
C	4	4	Template C*
D	3	4	1½″ × 7½″
E	1	4	1½″ × 1½″
F	1	4	2″ × 9½″
G	4	4	2″ × 2″

* Use Template C from Basic Pillow, Project 10.

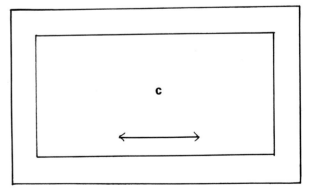

Full-size templates for Fruit Basket block. Inner line is seam line. Outer line is cutting line. Arrows indicate the straight grain of fabric.

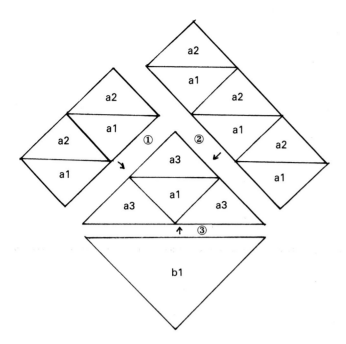

13–1   Diagram for seaming triangles and larger units of Fruit Basket block. Circled numbers indicate order of assembling units.

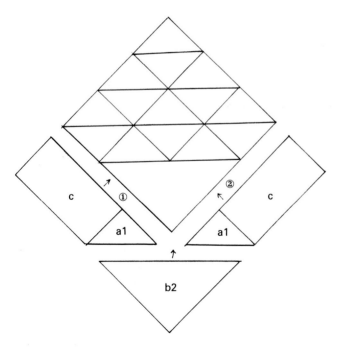

13–2   Completing the Fruit Basket block. Circled numbers indicate order of assembling units.

CONSTRUCTION

All construction is done with ¼" seam allowances. There are a number of seams to match, so piece carefully. The Fruit Basket replaces pieces A and B in the Basic Pillow (Project 10). The color distribution given here is based on the model (see photograph).

1. Take five triangles "a" of Color 1 (purple in the model; we will call these a1) and five triangles "a" of Color 2 (a2; white in the model). Seam each a1 triangle to an a2 triangle on its long side to make five a1/a2 squares. Set them aside for now.

2. Take another triangle a1 and attach it to an "a" triangle of Color 3 (a3; dusty rose in the model) on its long side to make an a1/a3 square.

3. Take two more a3 triangles and attach them to the a1/a3 square you made in Step 2, as shown in Figure 13–1, middle to make the pieced central triangle.

4. Attach two of the a1/a2 squares made in Step 1 together in a rectangle as shown in Figure 13–1, upper left. Attach the three remaining a1/a2 squares made in Step 1 together in a rectangle as shown in Figure 13–1, upper right.

5. Now assemble the two pieced rectangles and one pieced triangle as shown in Figure 13–1. The circled numbers indicate the order of piecing. For the third step, take a b triangle of Color 1 (b1) and attach it across the bottom on its long side to the pieced triangle. Set this unit aside for now.

6. Take two c rectangles and attach an a1 triangle to the short side of each, as shown in Figure 13–2.

7. Take the pieced square unit you assembled in Step 5 and, following the layout and order of piecing shown in Figure 13–2, seam the c/a1 units made in Step 6 to the sides of the pieced square unit. Add a b triangle of Color 2 (b2) to the bottom (see Figure 13–2).

8. Press the entire unit. The Fruit Basket block replaces pieces A and B in the Basic Pillow. To complete the Fruit Basket pillow top, follow the construction steps given in Project 10, starting with Step 2.

9. To complete the pillow, see instructions in Project 10 on "Completing and Stuffing a Pillow."

14. Single Wedding Ring Pillow

12″ × 12″ (30.5 cm × 30.5 cm)

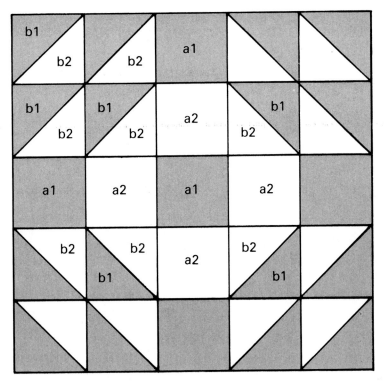

Diagram of finished Single Wedding Ring block.

The Single Wedding Ring design is usually used in a scrap quilt with a dark background. It offers a suitable block in which to try a negative color arrangement. Try black, navy, charcoal, or some other very dark color as the background. Use a medium to medium-light bright color for the design.

YARDAGE

PIECE	COLOR*	AMOUNT
a1, b1, D	1 (Dark brown)	¼ yard
a2, b2, F	2 (Medium warm tan)	¼ yard
C, E, G	3 (Pale orange)	⅛ yard
Pillow back	Your choice	⅜ yard
Batting	—	16″ × 16″
Muslin or batiste	—	16″ × 16″

* Colors in parentheses are colors in model.

CUTTING

PIECE	COLOR	QUANTITY	SIZE
a1	1	5	Template a
a2	2	4	Template a
b1	1	16	Template b
b2	2	16	Template b
C	3	4	Template C*
D	1	4	1½″ × 7½″
E	3	4	1½″ × 1½″
F	2	4	2″ × 9½ ″
G	3	4	2″ × 2″

* Use Template C from Basic Pillow, Project 10.

Single Wedding Ring Pillow.

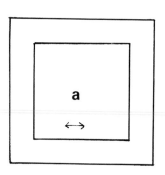

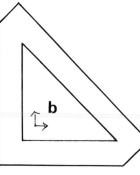

Full-size templates for Single Wedding Ring block. Inner line is seam line. Outer line is cutting line. Arrows indicate the straight grain of fabric.

CONSTRUCTION

The Single Wedding Ring block replaces pieces A and B in the Basic Pillow (Project 10). All construction is done with ¼" seam allowances.

1. Take 16 b triangles of Color 1 (we will call these b1) and 16 b triangles of Color 2 (b2). Join each b1 triangle to a b2 triangle on its long side (Figure 14–1) by sewing them with right sides of material facing, to form a total of 16 b1/b2 squares. Open them out and press them.

2. Take two of the squares made in Step 1 and join them together as shown in Figure 14–2, left, to make a rectangle. Make another rectangle exactly the same as the first one (Figure 14–2, right) and join them together to make a pieced square. This is the basic corner unit of the Single Wedding Ring block. It is rotated to form the pattern (arrows on Figure 14–4 show positioning of corner units).

3. Repeat Step 2 three more times to make the remaining three corner units.

4. Take an "a" square of Color 1 (a1) and an "a" square of Color 2 (a2). Assemble them into a rectangle as shown in Figure 14–3.

5. Repeat Step 4 three times to create three more a1/a2 rectangles.

6. Taking the units you created in steps 1 through 5 plus an extra a1 square, lay out the units and check their positioning with Figure 14–4. Follow the arrows on Figure 14–4 to orient the corner blocks. Numbers in circles indicate one possible order of sewing.

7. Using Figure 14–5 as a guide, complete the Wedding Ring block by sewing the three units made in Step 4 together. Be sure to match seams carefully. Press the block.

8. The Single Wedding Ring block replaces pieces A and B in the Basic Pillow (Project 10). For the rest of the pillow top, follow construction steps given in Project 10, starting with Step 2 (Figure 10–2).

9. To complete the pillow, see instructions in Project 10 on "Completing and Stuffing a Pillow."

14–1 A single square formed from two triangles. Numbers indicate colors.

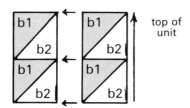

14–2 Sew the squares made out of triangles together.

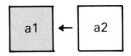

14–3 Assembling the rectangles from a1 and a2. Numbers indicate colors.

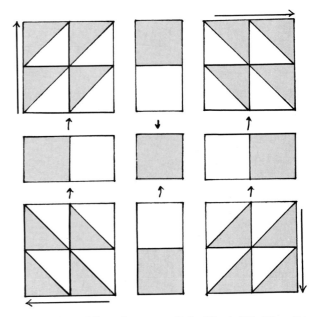

14–4 Assembling the parts of the Single Wedding Ring block into 3 units. Circled numbers indicate the order of sewing.

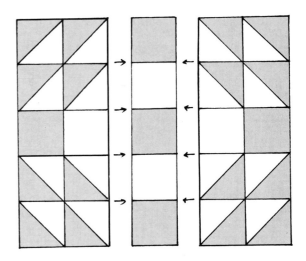

14–5 Joining the three units to form the complete block.

15. Evening Star Pillow

12" × 12" (30.5 cm × 30.5 cm)

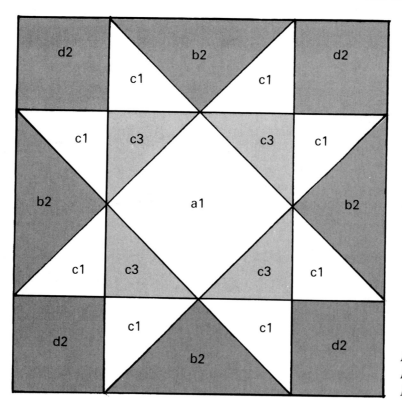

Diagram of finished Evening Star block. Numbers indicate colors.

The Evening Star appears to be very similar to the Ohio Star. They are somewhat alike, but are based on a different division of the square. The Ohio Star is based on a 9-patch design; the Evening Star is based on a 4-patch design.

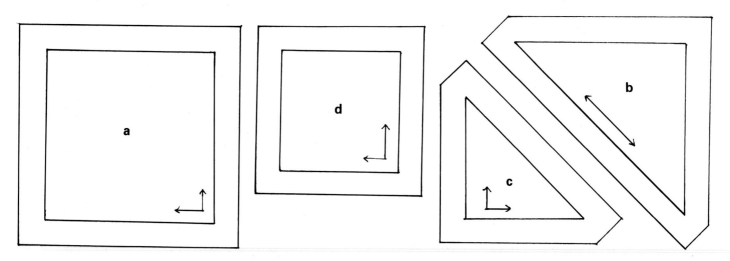

Full-size templates for Evening Star. Outer line is cutting line. Inner line is seam line. Arrows indicate the straight grain of fabric.

YARDAGE

PIECE	COLOR*	AMOUNT
a, c1, C, E	1 (Very pale blue)	⅛ yard
b2, d2, F	2 (Dark blue)	⅛ yard
c3, D, G	3 (Royal blue)	⅛ yard
Pillow back	Your choice	⅜ yard
Batting	—	16″ × 16″
Muslin or batiste	—	16″ × 16″

* Colors in parentheses are colors in model.

CUTTING

PIECE	COLOR	QUANTITY	SIZE
a	1	1	Template a
b	2	4	Template b
c	3	4	Template c
c	1	8	Template c
d	2	4	Template d
C	1	4	Template C*
D	3	4	1½″ × 7½″
E	1	4	1½″ × 1½″
F	2	4	2″ × 9½ ″
G	3	4	2″ × 2″

* Use Template C from Basic Pillow, Project 10.

CONSTRUCTION

The Evening Star block replaces pieces A and B in the Basic Pillow (Project 10). All construction is done with a seam allowance of ¼″.

1. First you will construct 4 rectangles like the one in Figure 15–1. Each is made out of one triangle b in Color 2 (dark blue in the model; we will call these b2) and two triangles c in Color 1 (triangles c1; pale blue in the model). To make each rectangle, attach each of the two c1 triangles by its long side to the short side of a b2 triangle. Press the 4 rectangles when completed, with seam allowances toward dark side.

2. Take two of the rectangles constructed in Step 1 and add d squares of Color 2 (d2) to both short ends of each rectangle, as shown in Figure 15–2. Set them aside for now.

3. Take square "a" (Color 1) and four c triangles in Color 3 (c3). Sew them by their long sides to the sides of square "a," as shown in Figure 15–3.

4. Take all the units you have created so far. Lay out the units as in Figure 15–4. Attach the two short rectangles (the ones without the d squares) made in Step 1 to opposite sides of the square unit that has "a" as its center (made in Step 3). Then attach the two long rectangles to the unit you just created. This completes the Evening Star block.

5. The Evening Star block replaces pieces A and B in the Basic Pillow (Project 10). For the rest of the Evening Star Pillow top, follow the construction steps given in Project 10, starting at Step 2 (Figure 10–2).

6. To complete the pillow, see instructions in Project 10 on "Completing and Stuffing a Pillow."

There are three colors indicated for the Evening Star block, but the design could easily be done with two colors. Just remember to keep contrast high between the star and the background to define the design.

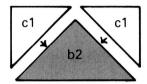

15–1 Attach long sides of c1 triangles to short sides of b triangle. Numbers indicate colors.

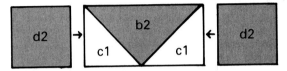

15–2 Attach d squares to c1–b–c1 unit.

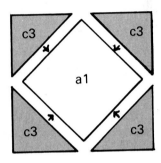

15–3 Attach c triangles to square "a" by the triangles' long sides.

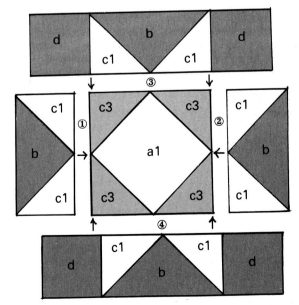

15–4 Carefully match seams, joining pieces in the order shown (circled numbers indicate the order of piecing).

Evening Star Pillow.

16. Eight-Point Star Pillow

12″ × 12″ (30.5 cm × 30.5 cm)

The Eight-Point Star is the basic format of a number of designs, including the Star of Bethlehem. The simple block design is actually less common than the Star of Bethlehem, a design that, when used in a bedspread, frequently covers the whole bed. The Eight-Point Star shown here is good practice for the more difficult Star of Bethlehem Pillow presented later (Project 17).

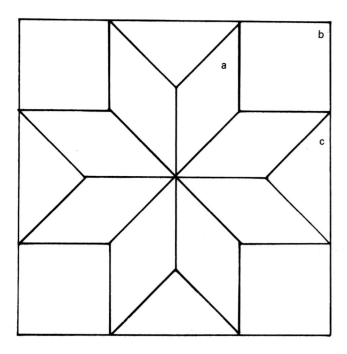

Diagram of finished Eight-Point Star block.

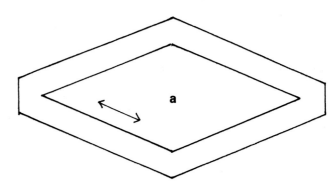

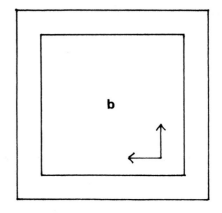

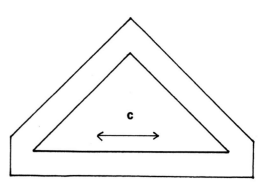

YARDAGE

PIECE	COLOR	AMOUNT
a, E	1 (Pink in model)	⅛ yard
b, c, C, F	2 (Purple in model)	⅛ yard
D, G	3 (Red in model)	⅛ yard
Pillow back	Your choice	⅜ yard
Batting	—	16″ × 16″
Muslin or batiste	—	16″ × 16″

CUTTING

PIECE	COLOR	QUANTITY	SIZE
a	1	8	Template a
b	2	4	Template b
c	2	4	Template c
C	2	4	Template C*
D	3	4	1½″ × 7½″
E	1	4	1½″ × 1½″
F	2	4	2″ × 9½ ″
G	3	4	2″ × 2″

* Use Template C from Basic Pillow, Project 10.

Full-size templates for the Eight-Point Star block. Outer line is cutting line. Inner line is seam line. Arrows indicate the straight grain of fabric.

CONSTRUCTION

The Eight-Point Star block replaces piece A and piece B in the Basic Pillow (Project 10). A seam allowance of ¼″ is used throughout the project.

1. Construction begins with the star itself. You will make 2 half-stars of 4 diamonds each. First take 2 diamonds "a" and stitch them together as shown in Figure 16–1, top left.

2. Add a third diamond "a," stitching from the center point out (see Figure 16–1), and a fourth diamond "a," also stitched from the center point out. You have now created a half-star.

3. Repeat steps 1 and 2 to make the second half of the star.

4. Now join the halves of the star (Figure 16–2), matching the center points carefully. Before sewing, pin or baste the halves together, right sides facing, to secure them. Press the star seams in a clockwise direction so that they lie flat when the unit is joined.

5. Following Figure 16–3, attach the four c triangles to the star, and then attach the four b squares. For each piece sewn, position the inner angle (right angle) of the square or triangle to be attached and stitch from the inner angle out on one side. Then go back to the starting point and complete the insertion by sewing the second side (see Figure 16–3). This completes the Eight-Point Star block.

6. The Eight-Point Star block replaces Piece A and Piece B in the Basic Pillow (Project 10). To complete the Eight-Point Star pillow top, follow the construction steps given in Project 10, starting at Step 2 there (Figure 10–2).

7. To complete the pillow, see instructions in Project 10 on "Completing and Stuffing a Pillow."

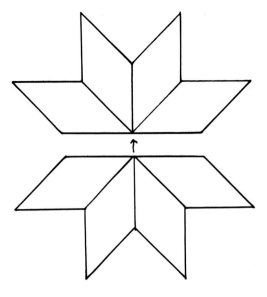

16–2   Attach the two halves of the star to each other, being careful to match the center points.

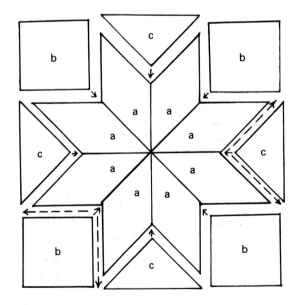

16–3   Attach the four c triangles and the b squares by sewing each side from the innermost point out, then sewing the next side, also from the inner point out. Dashed line indicates direction of stitching.

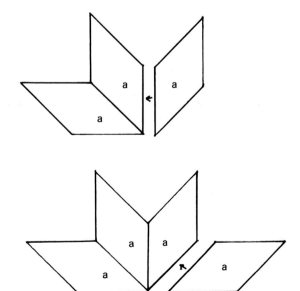

16–1   Top: attach the third diamond to the first two. Bottom: attach the fourth diamond as shown.

17. Star of Bethlehem Pillow

12″ × 12″ (30.5 cm × 30.5 cm)

The Star of Bethlehem, most commonly called the Lone Star by the "English," is popular with Amish people in every stratum. It is a variation on the basic eight-point star. In the Star of Bethlehem, each component diamond is divided into at least 3 × 3 rows and columns. The pillow top in the model has been matted and framed in a wide blue frame.

62

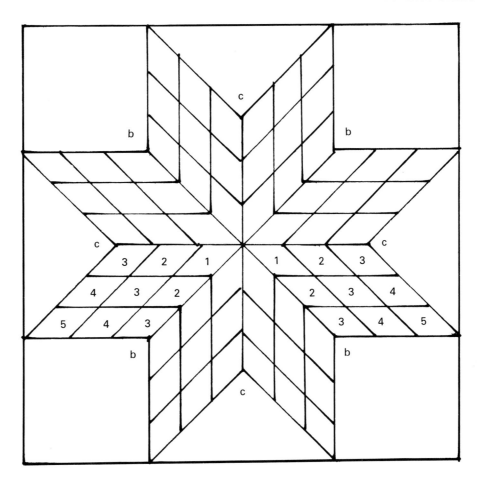

Diagram of the finished Star of Bethlehem block for pillow. Numbers indicate the colors to be used.

YARDAGE

PIECE	COLOR	AMOUNT
a	1	Scraps to make 8 of Piece "a" (or 4" × 6" total)
a	2	⅛ yard
a	3	⅛ yard
a	4	⅛ yard
a	5	Scraps to make 8 of Piece "a" (or 4" × 6" total)
b and c (Background)	Your choice	⅛ yard
D	Your choice	⅛ yard
E	Your choice	4" × 4"
F	Your choice	⅛ yard
G	Your choice	5" × 5"
Pillow back	Your choice	⅜ yard
Batting	—	16" × 16"
Muslin or batiste	—	16" × 16"

CUTTING

PIECE	COLOR	QUANTITY	SIZE
a	1	8	Template a
a	2	16	Template a
a	3	24	Template a
a	4	16	Template a
a	5	8	Template a
b	Your choice	4	Template b
c	Same as "b"	4	Template c
D	Your choice	4	1½" × 7½"
E	Your choice	4	1½" × 1½"
F	Your choice	4	2" × 9½"
G	Your choice	4	2" × 2"

CONSTRUCTION

Since the segment diamonds are small, you may elect to hand piece the Star of Bethlehem block. The Star block replaces pieces A, B, and C of the Basic Pillow (Project 10). All construction is done with seam allowances of ¼".

1. Study the diagram of the finished Star of Bethlehem block. You will see that it is made up of 8 large diamonds, each of which in turn is made up of nine little diamonds (of size "a"). The large diamonds meet at the center in Color 1.

2. Take nine small diamonds "a" as follows: one of Color 1, two of Color 2, three of Color 3, two of Color 4, and one of Color 5. From this we will create one large diamond. Following the color order shown in Figure 17–1, sew together 3 rows of 3 diamonds each.

3. Join the three rows by sewing as shown in Figure 17–1. When you have joined the 3 rows to make one large diamond (Figure 17–2), press the seams towards the outer point (that is, towards Color 5).

4. Repeat the procedure you followed in Steps 2 and 3 seven times more, to form a total of eight large diamonds that make up the Star of Bethlehem.

5. Now it is time to assemble the large diamonds. Join two large diamonds, matching their seams carefully. Begin your seam line at the center point of the star and sew outward (see Figure 17–3).

6. Join a third large diamond to the first two. Begin your stitching line at the center point, as with the previous diamond. Add a fourth large diamond, again beginning to sew at the center (Figure 17–4). Now you have joined four large diamonds, or half of the star pattern. Press the unit and set it aside.

7. Repeat steps 2 through 6 to form the second half of the star.

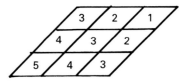

17–1 *Color layout of a large diamond for Star of Bethlehem pillow.*

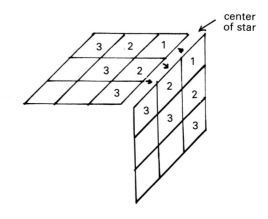

17–2 *Three rows joined to form one large diamond.*

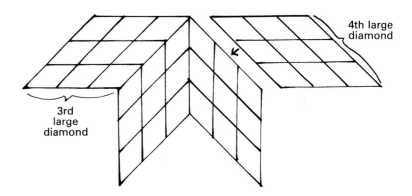

17–3 *Joining two large diamonds. Be sure to match seams carefully before sewing.*

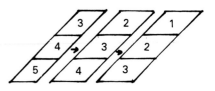

17–4 *Adding the fourth large diamond. Your center will be more accurate if you add a third diamond to one side of the first two and then add the fourth to the opposite side.*

8. Take your four c triangles. Double-check that your c triangles are cut with the grain line as indicated on the template for c. You will be borrowing trouble unless you have the straight grain of the fabric placed to lie on the edge of the star block. Recut c if necessary. Inset triangles c along the four sides of the star by pinning or basting them in place, matching the sides to the sides of each adjacent diamond, and then sewing them from the inner point outward on one triangle side and repeating the process on the other triangle side (Figure 17–5).

9. After you have set in all 4 triangles, you are ready to complete the block by setting in the b squares. Again stitch from the right angle outward, going back to the center of where the square joins the star to stitch the second side of the square (Figure 17–5).

10. Press your Star of Bethlehem block.

11. The Star of Bethlehem block replaces pieces A, B, and C in the Basic Pillow. For the rest of the Star of Bethlehem pillow-top, follow the construction steps given in Project 10, starting at Step 3 (Figure 10–3).

12. To complete the Star of Bethlehem Pillow, see the instructions in Project 10 on "Completing and Stuffing a Pillow." Otherwise, you may frame the pillow top, as you would a print, instead of making it into a pillow.

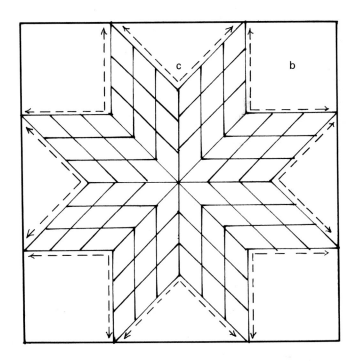

17–5 Attaching setting triangles and squares. Arrows indicate direction of sewing.

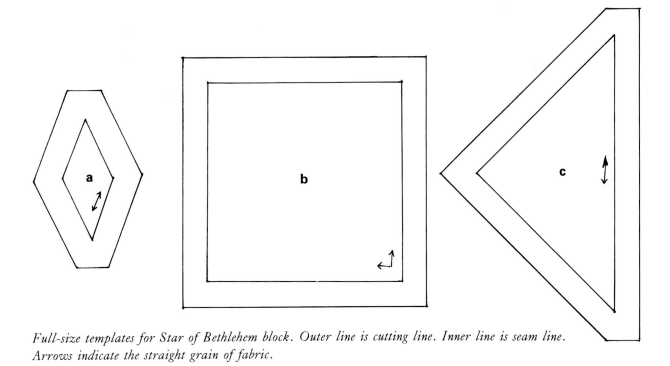

Full-size templates for Star of Bethlehem block. Outer line is cutting line. Inner line is seam line. Arrows indicate the straight grain of fabric.

18. Bow Tie Pillow

12″ × 12″ (30.5 cm × 30.5 cm)

The use of only solid-colored fabrics in Amish quilts results in bold graphics such as is seen in Bow Tie, a popular choice for young men's quilts.

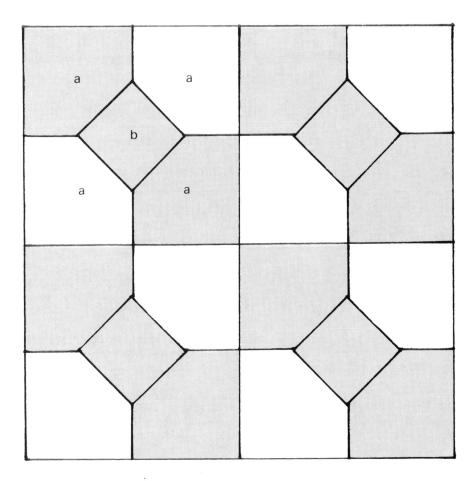

Diagram of finished Bow Tie block, showing positioning of pieces a and b.

YARDAGE

PIECE	COLOR	AMOUNT
a (background), C	1 (Very light blue)	⅛ yard
a and b (tie), D, G	2 (Purple)	⅛ yard
a and b (tie), E, F	3 (Royal blue)	⅛ yard
a and b (tie)	4 (Blue-green)	2″ × 6″
a and b (tie)	5 (Dark blue)	2″ × 6″
D	Your choice*	⅛ yard
E	Your choice	2″ × 8″
F	Your choice	⅛ yard
G	your choice	3″ × 9″
Pillow back	Your choice	⅜ yard
Batting	—	16″ × 16″
Muslin or batiste	—	16″ × 16″

* In the model shown, the borders D and F are close to but not an actual match to the colors of the small bow ties. Colors in parentheses are colors in model.

CUTTING

PIECE	COLOR	QUANTITY	SIZE
a	1	8	Template a
a	2	2	Template a
a	3	2	Template a
a	4	2	Template a
a	5	2	Template a
b	2	1	Template b
b	3	1	Template b
b	4	1	Template b
b	5	1	Template b
C	1	4	Template C*
D	Your choice	4	1½″ × 7½″
E	Your choice	4	1½″ × 1½″
F	Your choice	4	2″ × 9½″
G	Your choice	4	2″ × 2″

* Use Template C from Basic Pillow, Project 10.

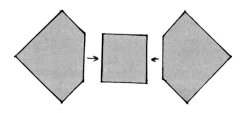

18–1   Making the bow tie unit.

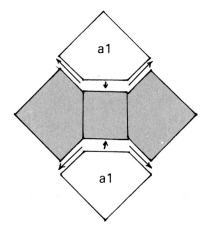

18–2   Attaching the background pieces. Long arrows indicate direction of stitching.

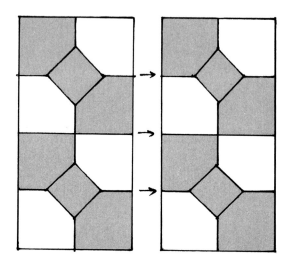

18–3   Join the squares into rectangles; then join the rectangles into a Bow Tie block.

CONSTRUCTION

The Bow Tie block replaces pieces A and B in the Basic Pillow. To create the Bow Tie block, you will assemble four squares (see diagram of finished block). All construction is done with seam allowances of 1/4".

1. Take two of Piece "a" of Color 2 (a2) and one of Piece b of Color 2 (b2). Sew the three parts together as shown in Figure 18–1 to form the first bow tie. (In our model, pieces "a" and b of a bow tie are of the same color.)

2. Repeat Step 1 with two of Piece "a" and one of Piece b for colors 3, 4, and 5, to form three more bow tie units.

3. Taking two of Piece "a" in Color 1 (the background color), follow Figure 18–2 to sew the "a" background pieces to the b square that forms the "knot" or center of a bow tie (created in Step 1). Then sew the angled seams that complete the unit, starting at the piece touching the knot of the bow tie and stitching out.

4. Repeat Step 3 with the three remaining bow ties until you have formed all four squares.

5. Carefully following diagram of the finished block, join the squares you created in steps 3 and 4 together in units of two and then join the units as shown in Figure 18–3.

6. Your Bow Tie block replaces pieces A and B in the Basic Pillow. For the rest of the Bow Tie pillow top, follow the construction steps given in Project 10, starting at Step 2 (Figure 10–2).

7. To complete the pillow, see instructions in Project 10 on "Completing and Stuffing a Pillow."

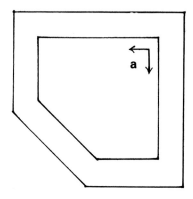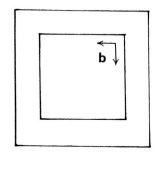

Full-size templates for the Bow Tie design. Outer line is cutting line. Inner line is seam line. Arrows indicate the straight grain of fabric.

19. Double Nine-Patch Pillow

12″ × 12″ (30.5 cm × 30.5 cm)

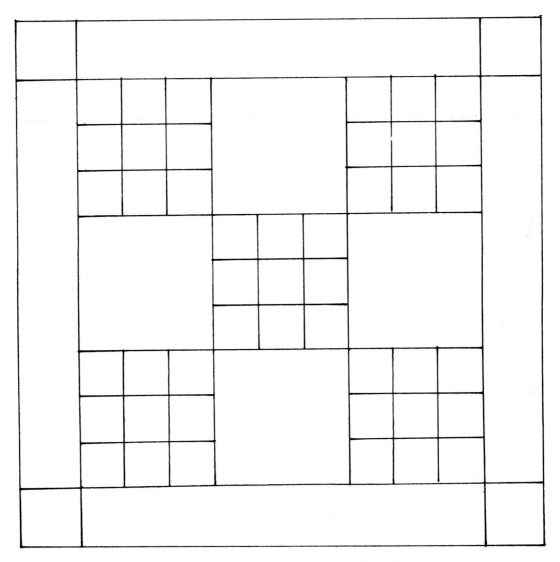

Diagram of finished Double Nine-Patch Pillow.

No design is more basic than a Nine-Patch. If you build a Nine-Patch block out of Nine-Patch Blocks, you then have a Double Nine-Patch. The model shown here is done in two colors, but three or more also may be used.

Double Nine-Patch Pillow.

This construction will introduce you to some quick piecing techniques involving sewn strips that are cut and used as piecing elements. Of course, if you prefer, you may piece the Nine-Patch block in the conventional method. The Double Nine-Patch block constructed here replaces pieces A, B, C, D and E of the Basic Pillow (Project 10). There are no templates provided for this construction—none are needed.

YARDAGE

PIECE	COLOR	AMOUNT
Pillow front pieces (design)	1 (White in model)	⅛ yard
Pillow front (background) and pillow back	2 (Black in model)	⅜ yard
Batting	—	16″ × 16″
Muslin or batiste	—	16″ × 16″

CUTTING

Using Color 1

1. Take ⅛ yard of material and cut in half to make 2 pieces, each of which is 4½″ × 22″.
2. For quick stripping, cut 3 strips, each 1½″ × 22″. You may have to cut the third strip from the second part of your ⅛ yard.
3. Cut 4 squares each 2″ × 2″. They will form the outer border corners (G in the Basic Pillow).

Using Color 2

1. Take ⅜ yard of material (13.5″ × 45″) and cut off a part 13.5″ × 14″ from the end for the pillow back. (The remaining piece should be 13.5″ × 31″.) Set the back aside for now.
2. From the remaining piece of Color 2, cut the following:

   - 3 strips, each 1½″ wide and 22″ long.
   - 4 squares, each 3½″ × 3½″. These will form the alternate blocks of the 9-patch design.
   - 4 strips, each 9½″ × 2″. These will form the outer border pieces (F in the Basic Pillow).

Color 1
Color 2
Color 1

Band I

Color 2
Color 1
Color 2

Band II

19–1   Create Bands I and II by seaming long strips of Color 1 and Color 2 together as shown.

CONSTRUCTION

1. Throughout the project, construction is done with ¼″ seam allowance, unless otherwise noted. We will now make two bands of 3 strips each. Take two strips of size 1½″ × 22″ of Color 1 and one strip 1½″ × 22″ of Color 2. Sew them together along their long sides so that Color 2 is in the middle, to form Band I, as shown in Figure 19–1, top.

2. Take two strips 1½″ × 22″ of Color 2 and one strip 1½″ × 22″ of Color 1. Sew them together along their long sides so that Color 1 is in the middle, to form Band II, as shown in Figure 19–1, bottom. Press both bands, keeping the seam allowance on the side of the dark color.

3. Take your gridded ruler. Take Band I and check its short edge for squareness, to be sure it is perpendicular to the long edge, that is, it makes a square corner like the corner of your right triangle. If it isn't perpendicular, straighten it by cutting off the part that extends over the square line with your rotary cutter (you can mark it first with a pencil or other marker).

4. Now that Band I is squared up, make ten 1½″-wide bars by slicing across the three stripes of Band I with your rotary cutter. We will call these bars "bar I," since they came from Band I. See Figure 19–2, top. Put these bars aside for the moment.

5. Take Band II, which you created in Step 2. Straighten the short edge as you did in Step 3 above. Then make five 1½″-wide bars by slicing across the three stripes of Band II (see Figure 19–2, bottom). We will call each "bar II" as it came from Band II.

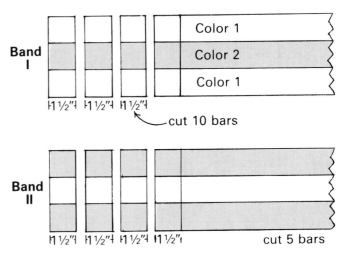

19–2   Create bars by slicing across all 3 colors in each band with rotary cutter.

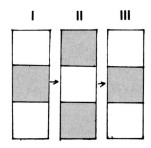

I   II   III

19–3   *Join three bars together (two Bar I and one Bar II) to form a nine-patch unit.*

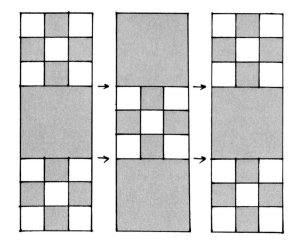

19–4   *Join the nine-patch units to large blocks of Color 1 (shaded) as shown. Then join the three units thus created into a double nine-patch.*

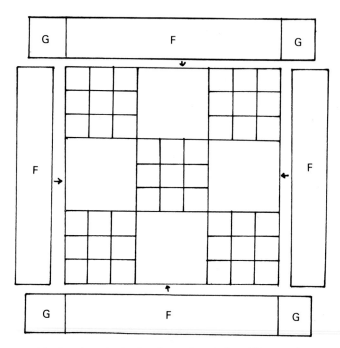

19–5   *Attach the border units of the pillow to the Double Nine-Patch block.*

6. Now take two of bar I and one of bar II. As shown in Figure 19–3, join them together to make a Nine-Patch unit. Be sure to observe your ¼″ seam allowances.

7. Repeat Step 6 four more times, so that you have made a total of 5 Nine-Patch units.

8. Take one of the 3½″ × 3½″ squares you cut out of Color 2. Sew a Nine-Patch block to the opposite ends of one Color 2 square, as shown in Figure 19–4, left. Then take two more 3½″ × 3½″ squares of Color 2 and attach a Nine-Patch block in between them, as shown in Figure 19–4, middle. Make the third unit by attaching the remaining two 3½″ × 3½″ squares to the opposite ends of a Nine-Patch block (Figure 19–4, right).

9. Join the three units of 3 blocks you made in Step 8 into a square, following the positions shown in Figure 19–4. This completes the Double Nine-Patch block, which is the central design of the pillow. It replaces pieces A, B, C, D, and E of the Basic Pillow (Project 10).

10. Take two 2″ × 9½″ strips of Color 2. These form Piece F of the Basic Pillow. Attach them to the sides of the Nine-Patch block as shown in Figure 19–5.

11. Take the two 2″ × 2″ squares of Color 1. They are pieces G of the Basic Pillow. Attach a square to each short end of the strip of Color 2 that is 2″ × 9½″ (Piece F) to form the G–F–G border unit (see Figure 19–5, top).

12. Repeat Step 11 to form the second G–F–G border unit.

13. Attach one G–F–G border unit to the bottom of the unit created in Step 10, as shown in Figure 19–5. Attach the other G–F–G border unit to the top of the unit created in Step 10.

14. This completes the Double Nine-Patch Pillow top. Press the pillow top.

15. To complete the pillow, see the instructions in Project 10 (The Basic Pillow) for "Completing and Stuffing a Pillow."

20. Bear's Paw Pillow

12″ × 12″ (30.5 cm × 30.5 cm)

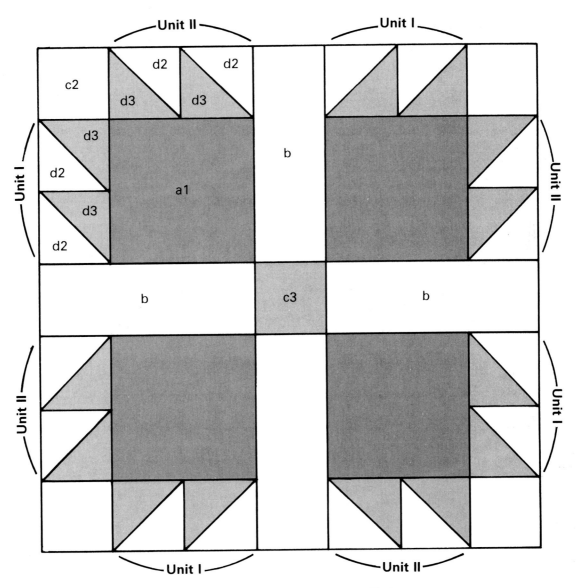

Diagram of finished Bear's Paw block.

The Bear's Paw design is another link with early American life, in which the sight of bear footprints on the ground was a common occurrence. Although this design appears more complicated than some of the other pillow blocks, looks are deceiving. There are very few seams to be matched in construction. The model shown is rendered in three colors. The Bear's Paw block replaces pieces A, B, and C in the Basic Pillow (Project 10).

73

Bear's Paw Pillow.

YARDAGE

PIECE	COLOR	AMOUNT
a, D	1 (Brown in model)	⅛ yard
b, c2, E, G	2 (Yellow in model)	⅛ yard
c3, d3, F	3 (Olive green in model)	⅛ yard
Pillow back	Choose one of the above	⅜ yard
Batting	—	16″ × 16″
Muslin or batiste	—	16″ × 16″

CUTTING

PIECE	COLOR	QUANTITY	SIZE
a	1	4	Template a
b	2	4	Template b
c2	2	4	Template c
c3	3	1	Template c
d3	3	16	Template d
d2	2	16	Template d
D	1	4	1½″ × 7½″
E	2	4	1½″ × 1½″
F	3	4	1½″ × 9½″
G	2	4	2″ × 2″

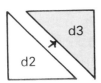

20–1 Seam a "d" triangle of Color 2 to a "d" triangle of Color 3.

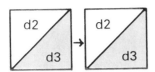

20–2 Create Unit I by joining two pieced squares as shown.

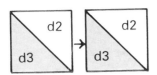

20–3 Create Unit II, a mirror image of Unit I.

CONSTRUCTION

The four "paw" sections are pieced first. All construction in the project is done with seam allowances of ¼". Each paw is constructed the same as the upper left one but is rotated ¼ circle (90°) more than the previous one around the center when assembled to make the design.

1. First take a "d" triangle of Color 2 (we will call this d2) and a "d" triangle of Color 3 (d3). Seam them together on their long sides, as shown in Figure 20–1. This will form a square that is a bear "toe" plus background.

2. Repeat Step 1 until you have formed 16 "toe" squares, each having a d2 and a d3 triangle. You can use chain-piecing methods (see Project 8) for joining the triangles into squares. Press the squares open, with seams toward the darker fabric.

3. As shown in Figure 20–2, make a Unit I rectangle out of two "toe" squares, being sure the colors are aligned as in the figure.

4. Repeat Step 3 to make a total of four of Unit I. (See Figure 20–0 for their final locations.)

5. Now seam together two of the remaining "toe" squares to form Unit II (Figure 20–3).

6. Repeat Step 5 to form three more rectangles of Unit II, for a total of four Unit II rectangles. You can see their final locations in the diagram of the finished Bear's Paw block.

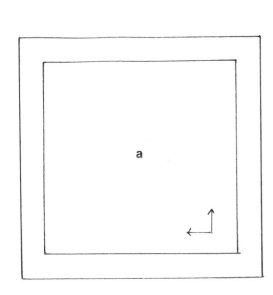

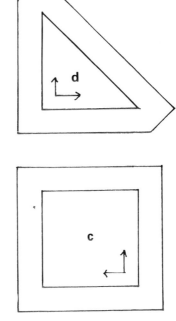

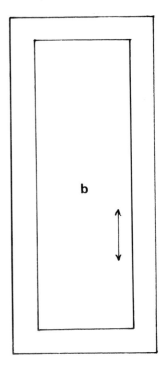

Full-size Bear's Paw templates. Outer line is cutting line; inner line is seam line. Arrows indicate straight grain of fabric.

7. Take your four squares of size c in Color 2 (c2). Following Figure 20–4 closely, attach each c2 square to a Unit II rectangle at the left of Unit II. The c2 square is always attached to a d3 triangle, never to a d2 triangle. We will call the combined unit c + Unit II.

8. Following Figure 20–5, join a Unit I rectangle to an a1 square as shown. Repeat this step three more times. We will call the unit formed Unit I + "a."

9. Attach the c + Unit II strip to the Unit I + "a" rectangle, as shown in Figure 20–5, to form the upper left paw.

10. Repeat steps 7, 8, and 9 three times to form the three remaining paw units.

11. Next you will form the inner strips that separate the paws. Take two b2 strips (b strips of Color 2) and attach them to opposite sides of a c square of Color 3 (c3) by their short sides (see Figure 20–6, middle) to make Panel II.

12. Lay out all the paw units, with the remaining b strip units between the top and bottom and Panel II vertically in the middle (see Figure 20–6). Be sure all units are oriented correctly.

13. Seam a b strip to the top left and bottom left paws, as shown in Figure 20–6, left, to make Panel I.

14. Seam the top right and bottom right paws to a b strip, as shown in Figure 20–6, right, to make Panel III.

15. To complete the Bear's Paw block, seam all three panels (Panel I, II, and III) together vertically.

16. The Bear's Paw block replaces pieces A, B, and C in the Basic Pillow (Project 10). To complete the Bear's Paw pillow top, follow the construction steps in Project 10, starting at Step 3 (Figure 10–3).

17. To complete the pillow, see the instructions in Project 10 (the Basic Pillow) on "Completing and Stuffing a Pillow."

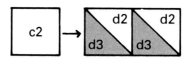

20–4   Join a c2 square to a Unit II, at left, keeping colors in position as shown.

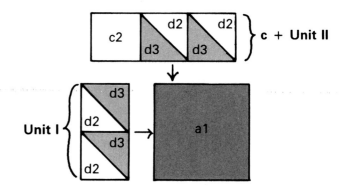

20–5   Join the Unit I rectangle to an "a" square. Join the c + Unit II rectangle.

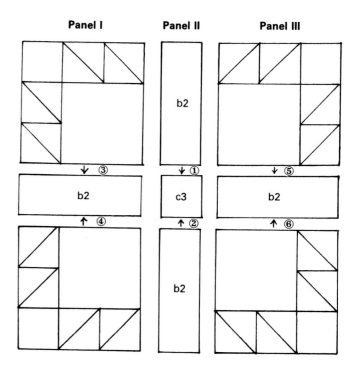

20–6   First piece the center panel (Panel II). Then join paw units to b strips as shown. Circled numbers indicate order of piecing.

21. Whole Cloth Pillow

12″ × 12″ (30.5 cm × 30.5 cm)

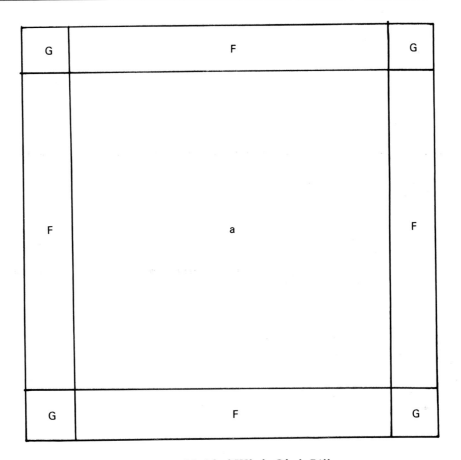

Diagram of finished Whole Cloth Pillow.

Whole cloth refers to a quilt top containing little or no piecing. Sometimes the Amish refer to these quilts as *plain quilts*. The design elements are contributed by the quilting motifs. A special feathered circle quilting design is provided to fill the center panel of the Whole Cloth Pillow (Figure Q16 in the quilting template section at the back of the book). Only a single border is indicated for this pillow. Amish quilts are rich with feathered designs. In fact, I don't think the design can be overused.

YARDAGE*

PIECE	COLOR	AMOUNT
a and G	1	¼ yard
F and Pillow back	2	⅜ yard
Batting	—	16″ × 16″
Muslin or batiste	—	16″ × 16″

* Note: A fabric-safe marker for transferring quilt design also is needed for this project; ½″ masking tape is recommended for use in the quilting stage.

CUTTING

PIECE	COLOR	QUANTITY	SIZE
a	1	1	9½″ × 9½″
F	2	4	2″ × 9½″
G	1	4	2″ × 2″
Pillow back	2	1	12½″ × 12½″

Whole Cloth Pillow.

TRANSFERRING A QUILT MOTIF

Before any sewing is done, transfer the quilting motif given in Figure Q16 to your center panel (Piece "a"). Try this:

1. Trace the design in Q16 with a medium-weight black felt-tip pen onto a 10" square of white freezer paper. (Draw on the side without the coating.) Be sure you have the design well centered on the 10" square.

2. Using an iron set on "cotton," with the coated side of the paper facing the wrong side of the material, press, centering the fabric square on the paper square. The heat of the iron will adhere the paper to the fabric. Now the design is in position and will not slip.

3. Depending on the color you have selected, you may be able to see the design through the fabric with no trouble. If not, you will need to get some light behind it. A lightbox, a tool frequently used by commercial artists, is a good solution. Since most quilters do not have a lightbox—especially not Amish quilters—you may need to improvise. The easiest makeshift lightbox is any good-sized clean window during daylight hours.

4. After you have attached your design paper to the cloth panel as described in Step 2, hold your prepared center panel "a" with the freezer paper against the window (or tape it there), with the fabric facing you. Trace your design onto the fabric with a fabric-safe marker; this ensures that the lines can be removed, if neces-

sary, when you finish quilting. You will be surprised to see that even very dark colors of material will allow the design to show through if they have the light coming through them. If your material is very dark, a white or silver-colored pencil may work better than a marker.

5. After your tracing of the design onto the material is complete, peel away the freezer paper.

CONSTRUCTION

After you finish transferring the quilting design to the central panel, as described in "Transferring a Quilting Motif," proceed as follows:

1. Complete the pillow top by attaching two border strips F to opposite sides of the central panel "a." Attach squares G to the short ends of each remaining border strip F. Then attach one unit G–F–G to the top of the central panel "a" and one unit G–F–G to the bottom of central panel "a." (See Figure 21–1 for layout.)

2. When pressing the pillow top, press the seams only— avoid pressing over your marked design; some markers will be set by heat and will not be able to be removed after that.

3. Cut your pillow top backing, muslin, and batting 2" larger in each dimension than your pillow top's unfinished size (so make them 14½" × 14½"). Hand baste the pillow top, batting, and muslin together. You are making a sandwich with the pillow top facing out, the batting in the middle and the muslin facing out on the bottom. Your basting will hold the three layers flat and snug while you quilt. I prefer basting first in a spider-web manner, always working from the central area to the outer edge, and then I superimpose a further rectangle grid of basting (Figure 10–5). The "spider web" eases the excess fullness out. The grid reinforces the positioning. Finally, run a line of basting completely around the edge of the pillow (or quilt) top about ⅛"– ¼" from the outer edge. Do not remove the basting around the edge, even after the quilting is complete. It will help control the edge while you complete the pillow.

4. Select quilting thread to match or blend with Color 1 (the color of Piece "a"). Before you complete the rest of your pillow, do the quilting of the central circle, as described in the quilting instructions at the back of the book (Quilt Stitchery). Do background quilting as described here in "Adding Background Quilting."

5. Once the quilting is done, follow the instructions in Project 10, the Basic Pillow, on "Completing and Stuffing a Pillow," starting with Step 3.

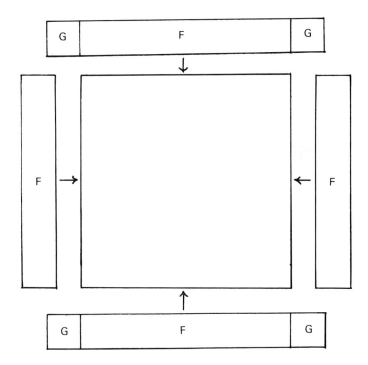

21–1 *Attaching border strips to center.*

ADDING BACKGROUND QUILTING*

This is a good opportunity to see how much background quilting will add depth and enhance your motifs. You can try adding lines across your feathered circle. To do this, you can use ½" wide masking tape. That will be the perfect width for quilting the background of the feathered design of the size given in Q16. Using tape eliminates the need to mark the background lines on the material.

After quilting of the circular center design is complete, place a length of masking tape on the diagonal of the center panel and quilt along both sides of the tape (see color photo for reference). Remove the tape, reposition it next to one of the quilting lines you just made, and quilt along the other edge of the tape. You may reuse the tape several times before needing a new piece. Do not quilt through the area already quilted with the feathered motif; only add the lines to the outside of the circle. If you quilt inside the circle, make the lines closer together, as in the model.

Because the above design covers a small area, your investment of time in quilting a pillow is minimal; however, I hope that completing the background quilting given here will convince you to spend the extra time necessary to quilt larger projects.

---

* For detailed quilting instructions see the quilting section at the back of the book.

22. Grape Basket Table Runner

19½" × 60" (49.5 cm × 152.4 cm)

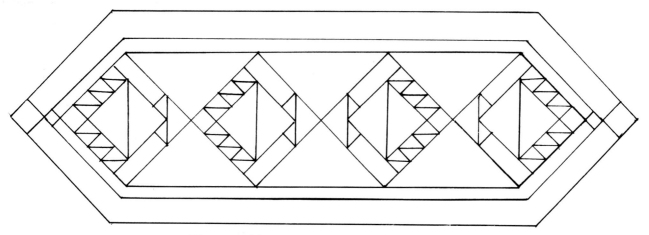

Diagram of finished Grape Basket Table Runner.

Using a table runner may be old-fashioned, but we hope the Grape Basket Table Runner will be fun for you nonetheless. It makes a beautiful wall hanging. The Grape Basket block is a likely choice for an Amish quiltmaker. The grape motif is one of the few life forms represented on Amish quilts. Quilting motifs for the setting blocks of the table runner (Figure Q13) are included in the quilting motif section at the back of the book.

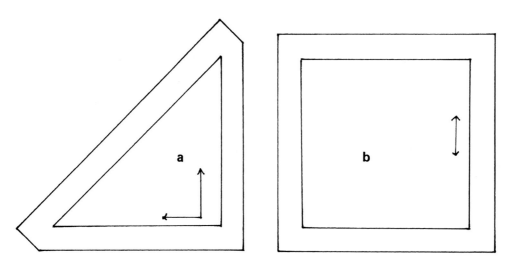

Above and on opposite page: full-size templates for the pieced Grape Basket Block. Outer line is cutting line. Inner line is seam line. Arrows indicate the straight grain of fabric.

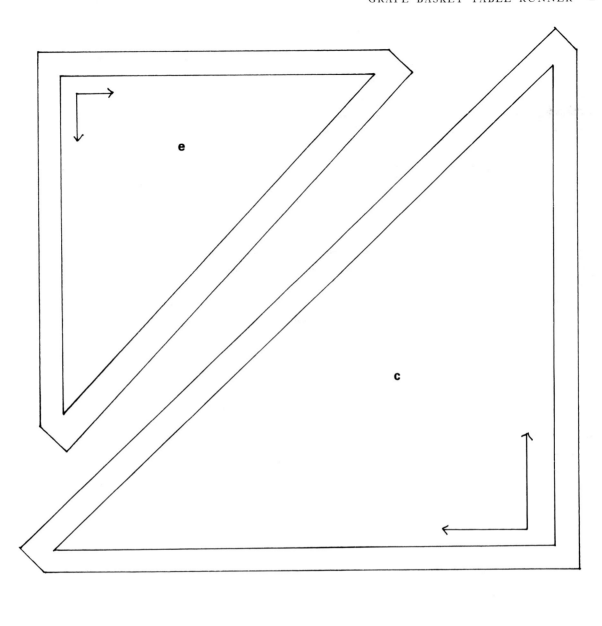

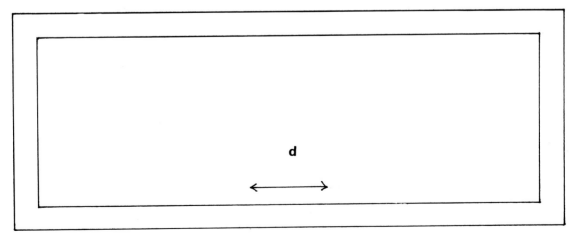

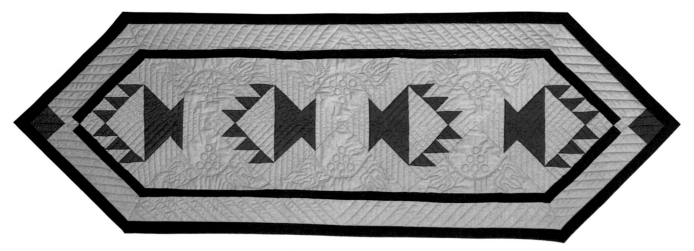

Grape Basket Table Runner.

YARDAGE

PIECE	COLOR	AMOUNT
Front of table runner	1 (Deep purple)	⅜ yard
	2 (Mint green)	⅜ yard
	3 (Orchid; light purple)	⅜ yard
	4 (Black)	½ yard
Backing	Your choice	1⅞ yards, cut to 24″ × 64″
Batting	—	24″ × 64″

CUTTING*

PIECE	COLOR	QUANTITY	SIZE
		LONG BORDER PIECES	
C	4	2	1½″ × 37⅝″
D	4	2	1½″ × 9¼″
G	3	2	3″ × 38½″
H	3	2	3″ × 10″
		PIECED GRAPE BASKET BLOCKS	
c	1	4	Template c
c	2	4	Template c
d	2	8	Template d
e	2	4	Template e
a	1	32	Template a
a	2	24	Template a
b	2	4	Template b
		SETTING BLOCKS	
B	3	6	9⅝″ × 9⅝″ right triangles**
		SHORT BORDER PIECES	
E	4	4	Template E
F	2	4	1½″ × 1½″
I	1	3	Template I
J	1	2	3″ × 3″

* Borders C, D, G, and H should be cut first to avoid needing to piece these long parts later. Then cut largest pieces needed in each color, and last do the smallest pieces in each color.
** Short sides of triangles go on straight grain of fabric. Short sides are 9⅝″.

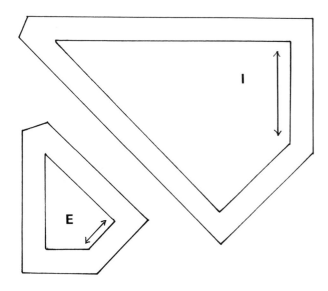

Full-size setting templates for border angles of Grape Basket Table Runner. Outer line is cutting line. Inner line is seam line. Arrows indicate the straight grain of fabric.

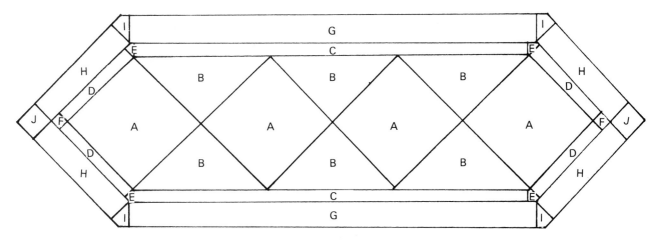

22–1   Piecing layout for table runner. "A" represents the 8¾″ × 8¾″ finished Grape Basket block (it is 9¼″ × 9¼″ including seam allowances).

CONSTRUCTION

All construction is to be done with ¼″ seam allowance. Study the piecing diagram, Figure 22–1. The squares labeled "A" in Figure 22–1 indicate where the Grape Basket blocks will go. First we will piece the four Grape Basket blocks.

1. For each basket, take six "a" triangles in Color 1 (we will call these triangles a1) and six triangles in Color 2 (a2). Seam one triangle of Color 1 and one of Color 2 together on the long side, with right sides of the material facing each other. This creates one of the six pieced small squares you need for each basket. Chain piecing may be used (see chain-piecing instructions in Project 8). Make five more a1/a2 squares.

2. Attach three of the squares created in Step 1 together in a rectangle, following the layout given in Figure 22–2 (top left). Attach a b2 square to the right end of this rectangle, keeping the a1 triangles at the lower right of each square in the rectangle.

3. Attach the three remaining small pieced squares you created in Step 1 together in a rectangle, as shown in Figure 22–2, top right. Note that in this rectangle, the a1 triangles are in the lower left of each square.

4. Take two triangles of size c, one of Color 1 (we will call this triangle c1) and one of Color 2 (c2). Sew them together on the long side to form a square, which will be placed as shown in Figure 22–2, middle.

5. Lay out all the units you made in Steps 2, 3, and 4 as shown in Figure 22–2. Double check their orientation.

6. Attach the rectangle on the upper right of Figure 22–2 to the c2/c1 square, as shown.

7. Attach the rectangle on the upper left of Figure 22–2, which includes the b2 block, to the unit you created in Step 6.

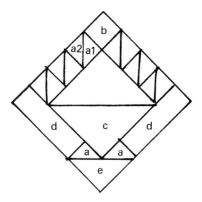

Diagram of finished basket.

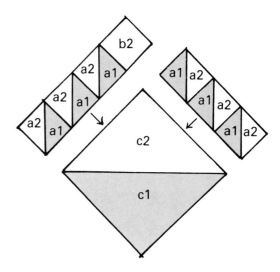

22–2   Attach the grape units as shown.

8. Now take two of Piece d of Color 2 (d2) and two of triangle "a" in Color 1 (we will call these triangles a1). Attach an a1 triangle to the short end of Piece d2. Attach a second a1 triangle to the second Piece d2 on the opposite short end (see Figure 22–3, bottom). This forms the bottom of the Grape Basket.

9. Attach the d2/a1 units formed in Step 8 to the pieced square formed in steps 1 through 7 (see Figure 22–3).

10. Take an e triangle and attach it to the bottom of the unit created in Step 9, as shown in Figure 22–4. This completes the first Grape Basket block, whose finished size should be 9¼" × 9¼" (dimensions include ¼" seam allowances).

11. Following steps 1 through 10 above, make three more Grape Basket blocks. Press each block with a dry iron.

12. Now take all 4 Grape Basket blocks and lay them out as shown in the diagram of the finished Grape Basket Table Runner. Note that the design is symmetrical; the two left-hand Grape Basket blocks have the "grapes" at the left and the two right-hand Grape Basket blocks have the grapes at the right. Take the six B triangles and lay them out as shown in Figure 22–5. Seam them to the "A" (Grape Basket) blocks as shown in Figure 22–5, until you have four units, as shown. Then attach the four units together. This completes the pieced interior of the table runner.

13. To start working on the inner borders, take the two C strips and attach them to the long sides of the center panel, as shown in Figure 22–6.

14. Take two D borders. Attach an F square to the short left end of one D border and attach an F square to the short right end of another D border (see Figure 22–6, top). Then attach an E piece so that the point is facing down on the remaining short side of each of the two D borders with the F squares (see Figure 22–6, top).

15. Take the two remaining D strips and the two remaining E pieces. Attach an E piece to the right side of one D strip. Be sure the point is facing up as shown in Figure 22–6, bottom. Attach an E piece to the left short side of the other D strip, being sure the point of the E piece is facing up.

16. To join the inner borders to the central block, first take the two E–D border units created in Step 15 and attach them to the main block, as shown in Figure 22–6, bottom.

17. Then take the two F–D–E border units created in Step 14 and attach them to the main block, as shown in Figure 22–6, top. This completes attachment of the inner borders. Now we'll proceed to the outer borders.

18. Take two of the G border strips. Seam one of the G strips to the bordered central unit you have created thus far, attaching one G border at the center top of the panel and one at the center bottom, as shown in Figure 22–7.

19. Take two H border strips. Attach an "I" piece to the right-hand short side of one H strip and attach another "I" piece to the left-hand short side of the other H strip, as shown in Figure 22–7, bottom. Be sure that the "I" pieces are both attached with the point facing up.

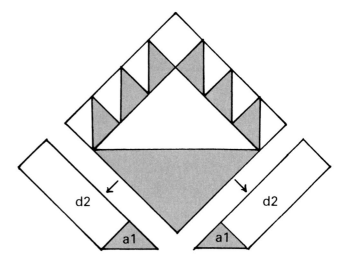

22–3 Attaching the bottom of the basket.

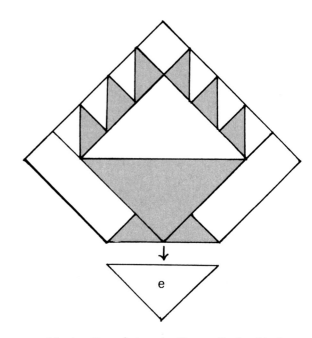

22–4 Completing the Grape Basket block.

20. Take two more H strips, the two remaining "I" pieces, and two J squares. Attach an "I" piece to the right-hand short end of one H strip and attach a J square to its other end, as shown in Figure 22–7, top left. Be sure the "I" piece has its point facing down. Take the second H strip and attach an "I" piece to its left-hand short side and a J square to its right-hand short side, being sure that the "I" piece has its point facing down (see Figure 22–7, top right).

21. Lay out all the pieces to be joined as shown in Figure 22–7. Following the order of steps numbered in the figure, attach the remaining outer border strips to the inner borders, as shown. (The G strips already were joined in Step 18.) This completes the table runner top. Press the entire runner.

22. To finish the project refer to quilting and binding instructions at the back of the book. The binding in the model is black.

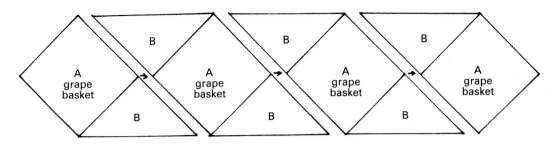

22–5 *Order of piecing of Grape Basket blocks and B triangles.*

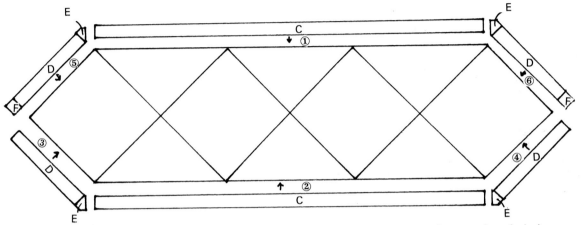

22–6 *Attaching inner borders to Grape Basket runner. Circled numbers indicate order of piecing.*

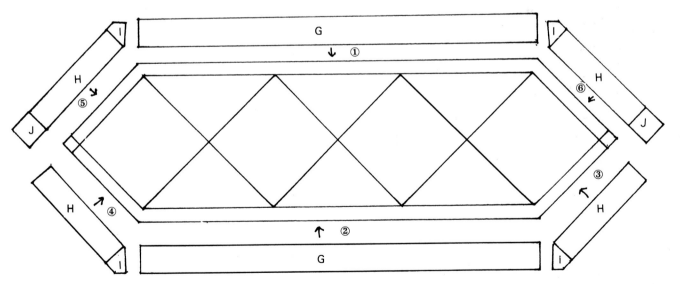

22–7 *Attaching outer borders to Grape Basket runner. Circled numbers indicate order of piecing.*

23. Sunshine and Shadow Quilt

26″ × 26″ (66 cm × 66 cm)

Sunshine and Shadow derives its name from the juxtaposition of light and dark colors that form concentric diamonds around a central square. For the full effect, there must be a range of light and dark materials to create the illusion of sun and shadow.

The "English" name for this quilt is "Trip Around the World." Traditional hand piecing of this design requires a full "trip" around the quilt, rather than piecing it in strips.

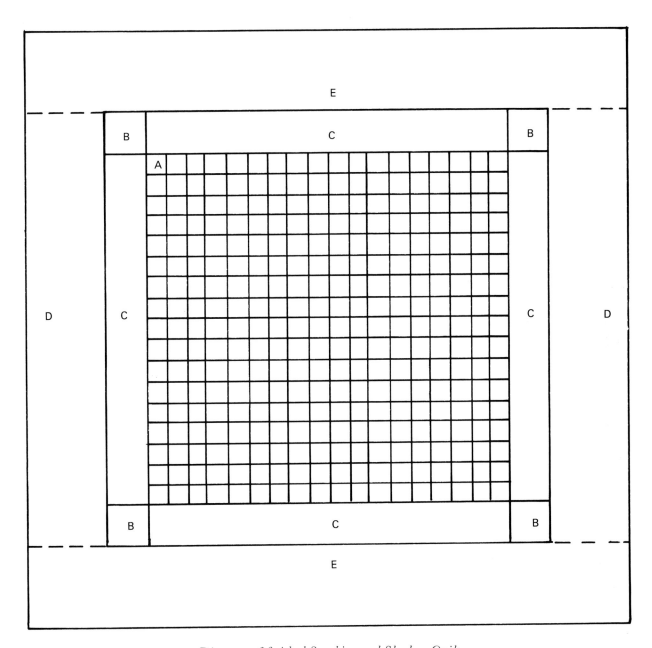

Diagram of finished Sunshine and Shadow Quilt.

There are 16 different fabric colors used in this wall hanging. Fabric 5, a medium dark, also is used for the inner border (C). Fabric 8, another medium dark, is used for the border corners (B). Fabric 1, used in the center, repeats at the four corners of the piecing. Fabrics 1 and 2 should be warm sun-catchers, like yellow, red, and orange. The rest of the fabrics should be a combination of lights, mediums, and darks in warm or cool tones, as suggested below.

YARDAGE

PIECE	COLOR*	AMOUNT
A, B	1 (Warm)	⅛ yard
A	2 (Warm)	⅛ yard
A	3 (Medium)	⅛ yard
A	4 (Medium)	⅛ yard
A, C	5 (Medium dark)	¼ yard
A	6 (Dark)	⅛ yard
A	7 (Dark)	⅛ yard
A	8 (Medium dark)	⅛ yard
A	9 (Light)	⅛ yard
A	10 (Light)	⅛ yard
A	11 (Light)	⅛ yard
A, D, E	12 (Dark)	⅝ yard
A	13 (Dark)	⅛ yard
A	14 (Dark)	⅛ yard
A	15 (Medium light)	⅛ yard
A	16 (Medium light)	⅛ yard
Backing and Type I binding	Your choice	31½" × 31½" or ⅞ yard
Batting	—	30" × 30"

* "Medium" refers to the darkness. It could be either a warm or cool color. Binding is formed from backing here.

CUTTING

PIECE	COLOR	QUANTITY	SIZE
A	1	5	Template A
A	2	4	Template A
A	3	8	Template A
A	4	12	Template A
A	5	16	Template A
A	6	20	Template A
A	7	24	Template A
A	8	28	Template A
A	9	32	Template A
A	10	32	Template A
A	11	28	Template A
A	12	24	Template A
A	13	20	Template A
A	14	16	Template A
A	15	12	Template A
A	16	8	Template A
C	5	4	2" × 17½"
B	1	4	2" × 2"
D	12	2	3½" × 20½"
E	12	2	3½" × 26½"

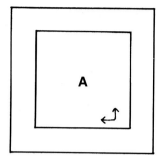

Full-size template for Sunshine and Shadow. Inner line is seam line. Outer line is cutting line. Arrows indicate the straight grain of fabric.

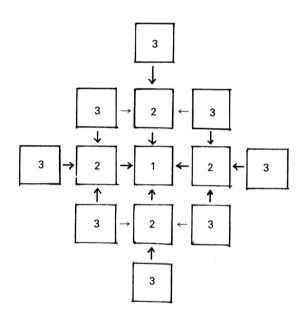

23–1 "English" method of hand piecing Sunshine and Shadow. Numbers refer to colors.

CONSTRUCTION

Hand Piecing (Trip Around the World)

If you wish to do the assembly by the hand-piecing "English" method, as is done for Trip Around the World, take an "A" square of Color 1, attach an "A" square of Color 2 to each side (all seaming is done with ¼" seam allowances), then add squares of Color 3 around that (Fig. 23–1). Proceed from the center of the design outward, following the color guide given in Figure 23–2, until you complete the entire center block. Then add the borders by hand or machine as described in steps 5 through 10 of the machine-piecing instructions given below.

Section I (9 × 8 squares)

1	16	15	14	13	12	11	10	9
16	15	14	13	12	11	10	9	8
15	14	13	12	11	10	9	8	7
14	13	12	11	10	9	8	7	6
13	12	11	10	9	8	7	6	5
12	11	10	9	8	7	6	5	4
11	10	9	8	7	6	5	4	3
10	9	8	7	6	5	4	3	2	←

Section II (8 × 8 squares)

10	11	12	13	14	15	16	1
9	10	11	12	13	14	15	16
8	9	10	11	12	13	14	15
7	8	9	10	11	12	13	14
6	7	8	9	10	11	12	13
5	6	7	8	9	10	11	12
4	5	6	7	8	9	10	11
3	4	5	6	7	8	9	10

↓ ↑

Section III (9 × 9 squares)

9	8	7	6	5	4	3	2	1	→
10	9	8	7	6	5	4	3	2
11	10	9	8	7	6	5	4	3
12	11	10	9	8	7	6	5	4
13	12	11	10	9	8	7	6	5
14	13	12	11	10	9	8	7	6
15	14	13	12	11	10	9	8	7
16	15	14	13	12	11	10	9	8
1	16	15	14	13	12	11	10	9

Section IV (8 × 9) squares

2	3	4	5	6	7	8	9
3	4	5	6	7	8	9	10
4	5	6	7	8	9	10	11
5	6	7	8	9	10	11	12
6	7	8	9	10	11	12	13
7	8	9	10	11	12	13	14
8	9	10	11	12	13	14	15
9	10	11	12	13	14	15	16
10	11	12	13	14	15	16	1

23–2 The four sections of the Sunshine and Shadow central design. Shaded block 1 is the center of the design. Numbers indicate colors.

1
2
3
4
5
6
7
8
9

23–3 Sample strip unit for pieced center column in Sunshine and Shadow. Numbers indicate colors of center strip.

Machine Piecing (Sunshine and Shadow)

1. If you choose the Amish way, you will find that piecing the design in sections, as suggested below, will help to simplify the machine piecing order. All piecing is done with ¼" seam allowance.

2. Study the diagram in Figure 23–2. The figure is divided into four sections. Each section may be further divided vertically into columns. In Section III the first column on the right starts with Color 1, the second with Color 2, the third with 3, etc. The other three sections also have an ordered progression of colors. In Figure 23–3 you see one column that makes up the basic unit of Section III. Not all columns are nine squares long, only the ones in sections III and IV. The ones in Sections I and II are only eight squares long. Following the color layout diagram in Figure 23–2, assemble your "A" squares into columns of 9 squares each for Section III. You can use chain-piecing techniques (see Project 8) to speed up construction. When you complete all nine columns, seam them together vertically to form the Section III square.

3. After you complete Section III, proceed to Section IV, assembling the squares into columns and the columns into a rectangle, following Figure 23–2 as a color guide. Assemble Sections I and II in the same way.

4. Once you have all four sections assembled, seam them to each other, matching centers and corners carefully.

5. To attach the borders, first stitch a C strip to the side of the central unit created in Step 4; then stitch another C strip to the opposite side of the central unit, following the layout in the diagram of the finished quilt.

6. Take the remaining two C strips and the four B corner squares. Attach a B square to the short ends of each of the two C strips.

7. Attach the B–C–B units created in Step 6 to the top and bottom of the central pieced unit assembled in steps 4 and 5.

8. Take the D outer border strips. Attach one to each side of the unit created in Step 7. See diagram of finished quilt for reference.

9. Take the two E outer border strips. Attach one to the top of the unit created in Step 8 and one to the bottom of the unit, using the diagram of the finished quilt as a guide. This completes your quilt top. Press the quilt top.

10. To finish the quilt, see instructions on quilting and binding at the back of the book.

24. Nine-Patch Barn-Raising Quilt

45" × 45" (114.3 cm × 114.3 cm)

The Nine-Patch Barn-Raising Quilt shown here was inspired by an Amish quilt made around 1925. The Nine-Patch is a very simple block to piece, but the arrangement creates a spectacular illusion of a transparent overlay of color. The 64 pieced blocks are identical; it is the juxtaposition of those blocks that works the magic.

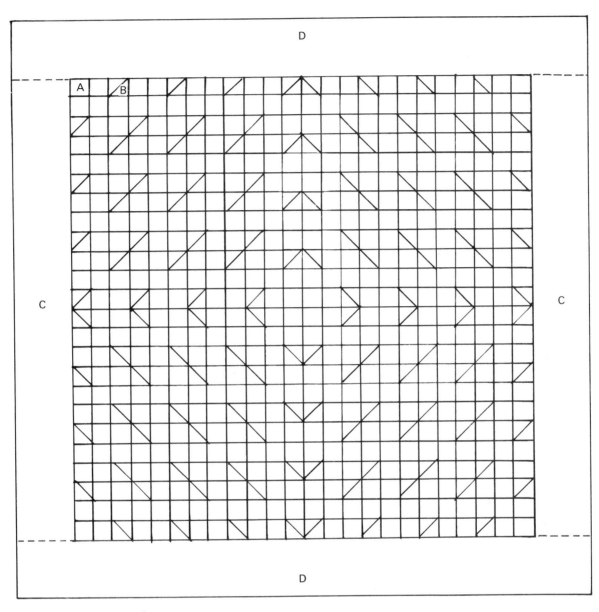

Diagram of finished Nine-Patch Barn Raising Quilt.

YARDAGE

PIECE	COLOR	AMOUNT
A, B, backing, border, and binding	1 (Pastel pink in model)	3 yards
A and B	2 (Black in model)	⅝ yard
A	3 (Purple-gray in model)	⅜ yard
A	4 (Very bright pink in model)	¼ yard
A	5 (Pale purple in model)	½ yard
Batting	—	47″ × 47″

CUTTING

PIECE	COLOR	QUANTITY	SIZE
A	1	64	Template A
B	1	128	Template B
A	2	64	Template A
B	2	128	Template B
A	3	128	Template A
A	4	64	Template A
Border C	1	2	5″ × 36½″
Border D	1	2	5″ × 45″
Backing	1	1	47″ × 47″
Binding	1	4	46″ × 46″

CONSTRUCTION

All construction is done with ¼″ seam allowance. The design is made up of 64 identical nine-patch blocks.

1. You have 128 B triangles of Color 2 (black) and 128 B triangles of Color 1 (pastel pink). We will subsequently refer to the black triangles as B2 and the pink triangles as B1. Take one B2 triangle and one B1 triangle and seam them together along their long sides (see Figure 24–1). This forms the B2/B1 square. Repeat this process until you have made a total of 128 squares. You can use chain-piecing methods (see Project 8) to speed construction. Press the squares open.

2. You are now ready to piece the 64 identical Nine-Patch squares that make up the design. You can use chain piecing to speed things along. To make one square, take the 7 small ("A") squares that make up one Nine-Patch block, along with two of the pieced B2/B1 squares you created in Step 1. Follow the color guide in Figure 24–2. Piece three columns of three squares each, following the layout in Figure 24–3.

3. Once you have finished your three columns, seam them together to form a Nine-Patch square, as is shown in Figure 24–3.

4. Repeat steps 2 and 3 until you have created a total of 64 Nine-Patch squares.

5. Now you are ready to piece the blocks together. You will assemble one-quarter of the entire design at a time (see Figure 24–4). Later you will assemble the quarters. Note that the blocks are not all oriented the same way in the quarter. Some have the Color 2 square (A2, black in our model), at the upper left, and some have the A2 square in another position (see Figure 24–5). Lay out all the blocks for the quarter, verifying their orientation with Figure 24–5.

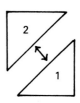

24–1 Join triangles on long sides.

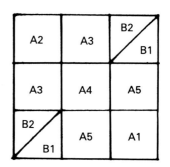

24–2 The nine-patch block. Numbers indicate colors.

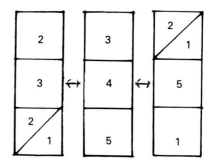

24–3 Seam the columns of three squares together to make the nine-patch unit, matching seams. Numbers indicates color.

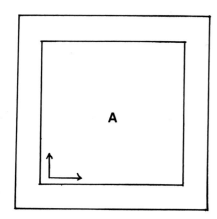

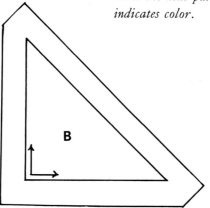

Full-size templates for Nine-Patch Barn Raising Quilt. Inner line is seam line. Outer line is cutting line. Arrows indicate the straight grain of fabric.

one block unit →

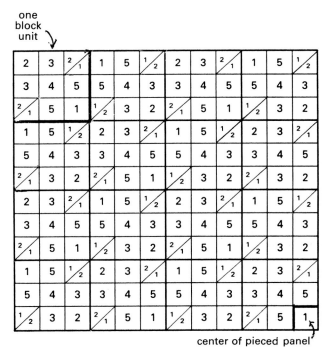

center of pieced panel

24–4 *Layout of upper left quarter of nine-patch design.*
Numbers indicate colors.

6. Following your quarter-design layout, piece the top left block to the next block in that row, then proceed to join the other two blocks in that row until you have attached all four together.

7. Piece the next three rows of blocks in the quarter-design layout.

8. Join the four rows to form the upper-left quarter design. Be sure to double-check the rows' orientation.

9. Following the instructions in steps 2 through 8, create three more quarters exactly like the first one.

10. Once you have completed all 4 quarters, lay them out as indicated in Figure 24–6. Note orientation of blocks 1 and 16 and be sure they are correctly placed. (Each quarter is rotated ¼ circle (90°) from the previous one to create the pattern.) Seam the quarters together, matching the centers carefully. This completes the central design of the Nine-Patch Barn Raising Quilt. Press the central design.

11. For border attachment, take the short borders (C) and seam them to the sides of the pieced central design (see diagram of finished quilt). Then attach the D borders at the top and bottom of the unit and press the unit. This completes the quilt top.

12. To complete the project, see quilting and binding instructions at the back of the book.

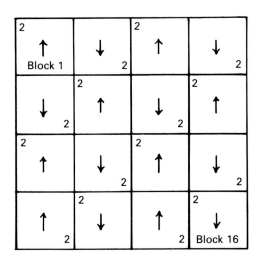

24–5 *Positioning of nine-patch squares in*
upper left quarter section of quilt. Note
position of Block 1 and Block 16. "2"
refers to Color 2.

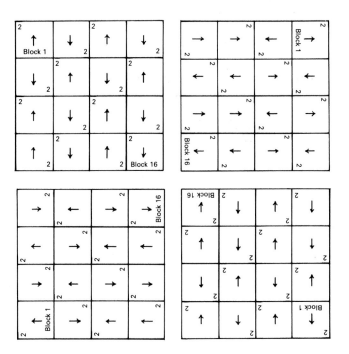

24–6 *Orientation of the four quarters of the quilt design*
for the Nine-Patch Barn Raising Quilt. Note location of
Block 16 in each quarter.

25. Ocean Waves Quilt

35″ × 35″ (88.9 cm × 88.9 cm)

Ocean Waves is one of the single-template patterns popular with Amish quiltmakers. It allows the quiltmaker to cut scraps as they are available and use them at another time. Setting Ocean Waves with black fabric, as is shown in the model, intensifies the jewel-like appeal of the multiple rich colors. The black provides sharp, vibrant contrast.

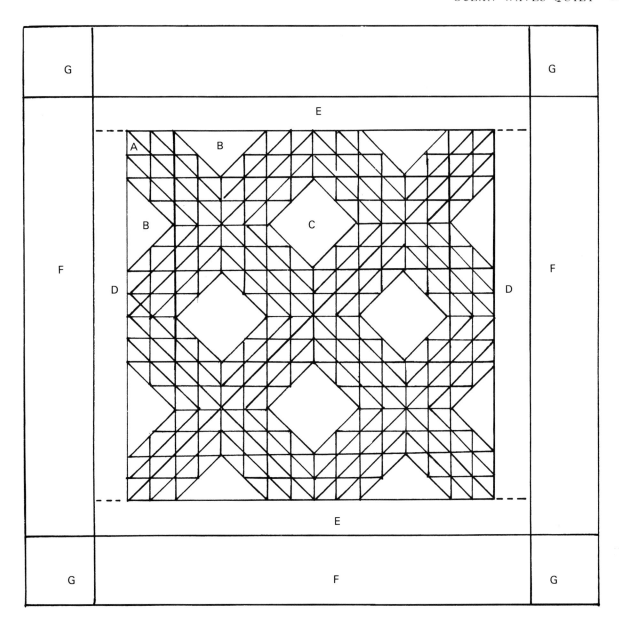

Diagram of finished Ocean Waves Quilt.

YARDAGE

PIECE	COLOR	AMOUNT
A	1 through 16	⅛ yard of each color, or scraps that total approximately 2 yards
B, C, F	Black	⅞ yard (31.5″)
D, E, and G	Your choice (turquoise blue in model)	⅞ yard
Back	Your choice	1¼ yard (trim to 39″ × 39″)
Batting	—	40″ × 40″

Note: a silver pencil for drawing on black is also helpful for this project.

CUTTING

PIECE	COLOR	QUANTITY	SIZE
A	1 through 16	384 (24 each of 16 colors)	Template A
B	Black	8	Template B
C	Black	4	Template C
D	Your choice	2	2½″ × 23½″
E	Your choice	2	2½″ × 27½″
F	Black	4	4½″ × 27½″
G	Your choice	4	4½″ × 4½″

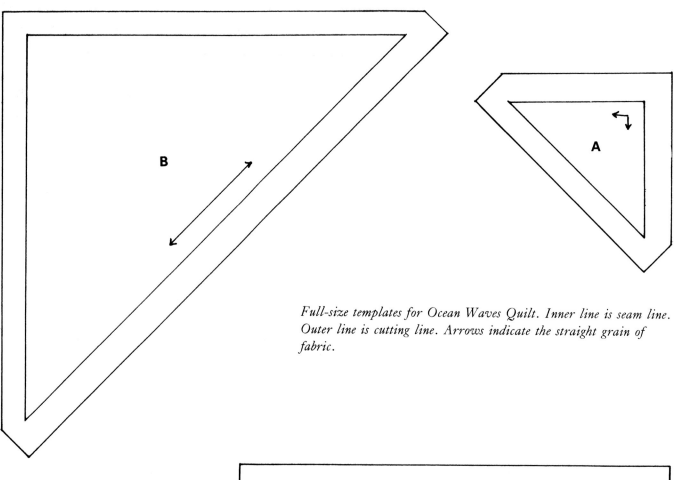

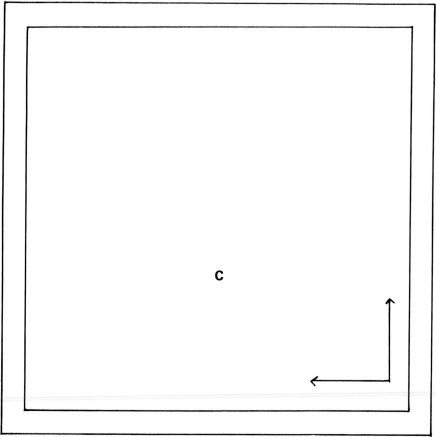

Full-size templates for Ocean Waves Quilt. Inner line is seam line. Outer line is cutting line. Arrows indicate the straight grain of fabric.

A custom quilting motif (Figure Q12, bottom) for the C parts (setting squares) of the quilt can be found in the quilt motifs section at the back of the book. A light box would be helpful for transferring the quilting designs (see Project 21).

CONSTRUCTION

All sewing is done with ¼" seam allowance. First we will create the main wave units, which comprise the Ocean Waves pattern. (You can see the shape of a wave unit in Figure 25–2, right.) Each wave unit is made of 24 A triangles. There are a total of 16 wave units.

MAIN DESIGN

1. Select 24 "A" triangles at random from your total of 384 "A" triangles. Make ten squares by seaming two triangles together on their long sides (see Figure 25–1). Do not join two triangles of the same color in a square. Chain-piecing techniques (see description in Project 8) will speed up construction. After making your ten squares, you will have 4 extra triangles left of the 24.

2. Attach the square units you created in Step 1 to each other, as shown in Figure 25–2, left. First you need to make two 2-square-long rectangles and two 3-square-long rectangles.

3. Attach an "A" triangle to one end only of each rectangle you created in Step 2 (see Figure 25–2, left). This uses up the extra triangles you had in Step 1. Be sure that each triangle is attached so that its long side is parallel to the long sides of the triangles seamed in the rectangles.

4. Following Figure 25–2, left, lay out and seam together the four units you created in Step 3, being sure that the parts are aligned correctly. This completes one entire wave unit.

5. Repeat steps 1 through 4 for 15 more times to create a total of 16 wave units.

6. Next, seam four wave units to a central setting square C, and then to each other, as shown in Figure 25–3. This creates an eight-sided unit, or octagon.

7. Repeat Step 6 to form a second octagon unit.

8. Attach the two octagon units created in steps 6 and 7 to each other, as shown in Figure 25–4, middle. Then attach a B triangle to the upper, outer corner of each of the octagons (see Figure 25–4, middle). This creates Unit II.

9. Take four more wave units and seam them together as shown in Figure 25–4, top. Take 2 B triangles and attach a B triangle in each of the two triangular spaces between the wave units that you just joined together. Attach a C square below the wave units. This creates Unit I (see Figure 25–4, top).

10. Repeat Step 9 to create a second grouping of four wave units, two triangles, and a C unit. Turn it upside down to be the basis of Unit III in Figure 25–4. Add two more B triangles to the upper, outer corners as shown in Figure 25–4, bottom.

25–1 Join two A triangles together on their long sides to form a square.

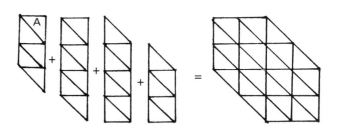

25–2 Join rectangles with triangles at their ends (left) to form a completed wave unit (right).

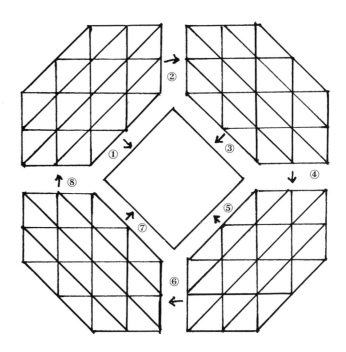

25–3 Join four wave units to a C square and to each other to form an octagon unit. Circled numbers indicate order of piecing.

11. For your final step of work on the central panel, assemble Units I, II, and III, following Figure 25–4 as a guide. Be sure to match the seams at pivot points. Do not stitch across the seam allowances.

Attaching the Borders

To attach the borders, follow the diagram of the finished quilt.

12. First attach the D border strips to the opposite sides of the central design you completed in Step 11 (Figure 25–5).
13. Then attach the E borders to the top and bottom of the central design.
14. Sew a G square to each end of two F border pieces.
15. Attach the two remaining F borders to the two opposite sides of the unit you created in Step 13 (Figure 25–6).
16. Attach the G–F–G border units to the top and bottom of the unit created in Step 15. This completes the quilt top. Press the quilt top.
17. To complete the project, see quilting and binding instructions at the back of the book.

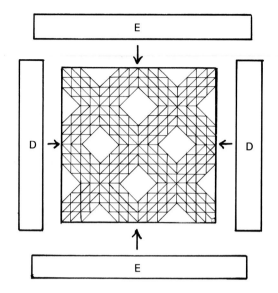

25–5 Attaching inner borders.

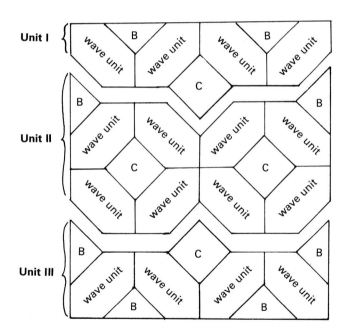

25–4 The three large units that make up the Ocean Waves panel.

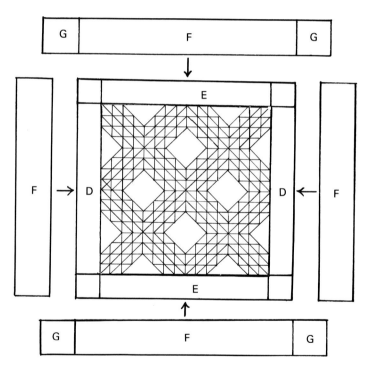

25–6 Attaching outer borders.

26. Mini Grape Basket Doll's Quilt

20″ × 20″ (50.8 cm × 50.8 cm)

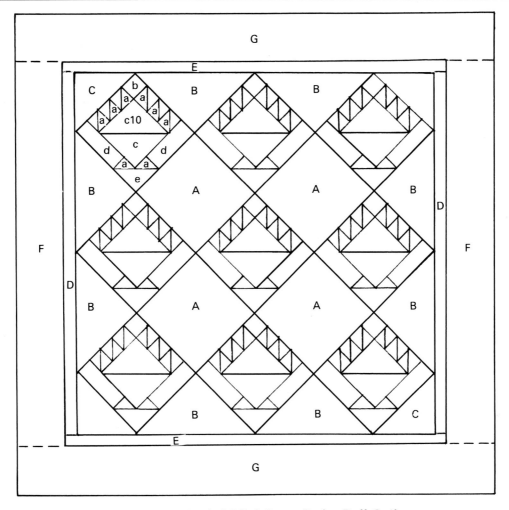

Diagram of finished Mini Grape Basket Doll Quilt.

This project will make a stunning small wall hanging as well as a doll quilt. There are nine pieced blocks, each with a different color basket, but all use black as background. The project requires a very small amount of each color; perhaps your scraps will be ample. The design was based on the measure of the diagonal of the blocks. Templates are provided for piecing the Mini Grape Basket block. A very bright electric blue was selected for the first border. In our model, more than one black fabric was used in the background and in the alternate blocks. This enriches the texture and reflects what might commonly happen when black scraps from more than one dress or project are combined; however, it is not absolutely necessary for your quilt. Quilting motifs for alternate blocks (A) and the borders (F and G) are included in the quilting motif section at the back of the book (Q3 and Q9).

Mini Grape Basket Doll's Quilt.

YARDAGE

PIECE	COLOR	AMOUNT
a (of basket), c (of basket)	1 through 9	at least 9″ × 9″ *of each color*
a, c, e (background of pieced blocks); B, C, F, G	10 (Black in model)	¾ yard
D and E	11* (Electric blue in model)	⅛ yard
Backing	Your choice	24″ × 24″
Batting	—	24″ × 24″

* Or use the color of one of the baskets, as in the model.

CUTTING

PIECE	COLOR	QUANTITY	SIZE
		BASKETS	
a	1 through 9	8 of each color (total 72)	Template a
a	10	54	Template a
b	10	9	Template b
c	1 through 9	1 of each color	Template c
c10	10	9	Template c
d	10	18	Template d
e	10	9	Template e
		SETTING BLOCKS	
A	10	4	Template A
B	10	8	Template B
C	10	4	Template C
		BORDERS	
D	11	2	1" × 15½"
E	11	2	1" × 16"
F	10	2	2½" × 16"
G	10	2	2½" × 20½"

CONSTRUCTION

All construction is to be done with ¼" seam allowance. Since the pieces are quite small, you may want to piece them by hand. You may also want to trim seam allowances to ⅛" to reduce bulk. Study the finished quilt diagram to get an overall view of the project. First we will piece the nine Mini Grape Basket blocks.

1. For each basket, take six "a" triangles in the color of that basket (one of the colors 1 through 9, depending on which basket you are working on). We will call these triangles "a." Also take six "a" triangles in Color 10 (the background color; we will call these triangles a10). Seam one "a" triangle of the color of your basket and one a10 triangle together on the long side. This creates one of the six pieced small squares you need for each basket (see Figure 26–1, left). Chain piecing may be used (see chain-piecing instructions in Project 8, Double Irish Chain) if you do not hand piece. Continue to create a total of six a/a10 squares in the same manner.

2. Attach three of the squares created in Step 1 together in a rectangle, following the layout given in Figure 26–1, right. Attach a "b" square in Color 10 (we will call this b10) to the right end of this rectangle, keeping the "a" triangles at lower right of each square in the rectangle (see Figure 26–1, right). We will call the unit created Unit I.

3. Attach the three remaining small pieced squares you created in Step 1 together in a rectangle, as shown in Figure 26–2, top right. Note that in this rectangle, the "a" triangles are in the lower left of each square. We will call this Unit II.

4. Take two triangles of size c, one of the color of the basket (we will call this triangle c) and one of Color 10 (triangle c10). Sew them together on the long side with right sides of material facing each other to form a square, which will be placed as shown in Figure 26–2, middle.

5. Lay out all the units you made in Steps 2, 3, and 4 as shown in Figure 26–2. Double-check their orientation.

6. Attach Unit II (the rectangle on the upper right of Figure 26–2) to the c10/c square, as shown.

7. Attach Unit I (on the upper left of Figure 26–2) to the unit you created in Step 6.

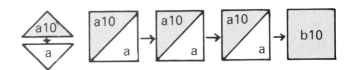

26–1 Left: Pieced square unit for Mini Grape Basket. Right: attaching three pieced squares to a solid square to make Unit I. Numbers indicate colors.

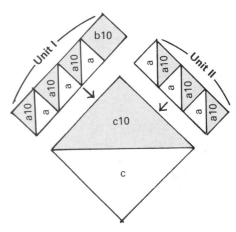

26–2 Attach Unit I and Unit II to pieced c10/c square.

8. Now take two of Piece d, Color 10 (d10), and two of Piece "a" in the color of the basket. Attach an "a" triangle to the short end of Piece d10. Attach a second "a" triangle to the second d10 rectangle on the opposite short end (see Figure 26–3, bottom). This forms the bottom of the Mini Grape Basket.

9. Attach the d10/a unit formed in Step 8 to the pieced square formed in Steps 1 through 7 (see Figure 26–3).

10. Take an e triangle in Color 10 (e10) and attach it to the bottom of the unit created in Step 9, as shown in Figure 26–4. This completes the first Mini Grape Basket block.

11. Using a different one of the colors 2 through 9 for the "basket" parts of each basket, follow steps 1 through 10 above to create eight more Mini Grape Basket blocks. Press each block.

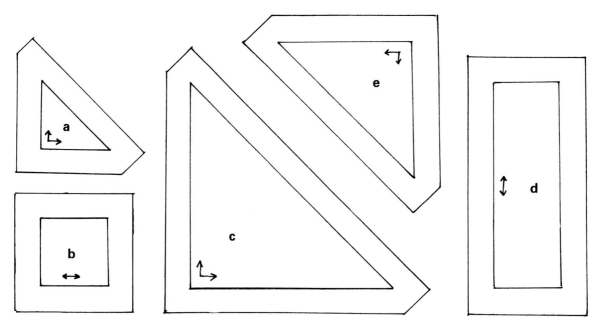

Full-sized templates for the Mini Grape Basket block. Inside line is seam line. Outside line is cutting line. Arrows indicate the straight grain of fabric.

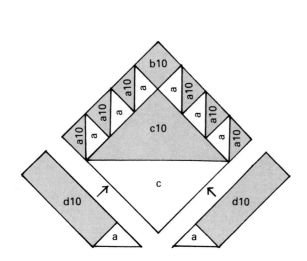

26–3   Attach d10/"a" unit to make bottom of basket.

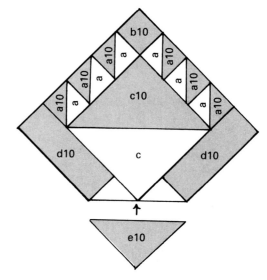

26–4   Attach e10 triangle to complete the pieced block.

12. Now take all 9 Mini Grape Basket blocks and lay them out as shown in the diagram of the finished quilt. Take 8 B triangles, 4 C triangles, and 4 "A" setting blocks (all of Color 10) and lay them out as shown in Figure 26–5. Seam them together as shown in Figure 26–5. This completes the pieced interior of the Mini Grape Basket Quilt.

13. To start working on the inner borders, take the two D strips and attach them to the sides of the center panel, as shown in the diagram of the finished quilt.

14. Take the two E strips. Attach one to the top of the unit created in Step 13 and one to the bottom.

15. Take two of the F border strips. Seam one of the F strips to each side of the central unit you have created thus far.

16. Take two G border strips. Attach them to the top and bottom of the unit made in Step 15, as shown in the diagram of the finished quilt. This completes the construction of the Mini Grape Basket Doll's Quilt top. Press the entire runner.

17. To complete the project, see quilting and binding instructions at the back of the book.

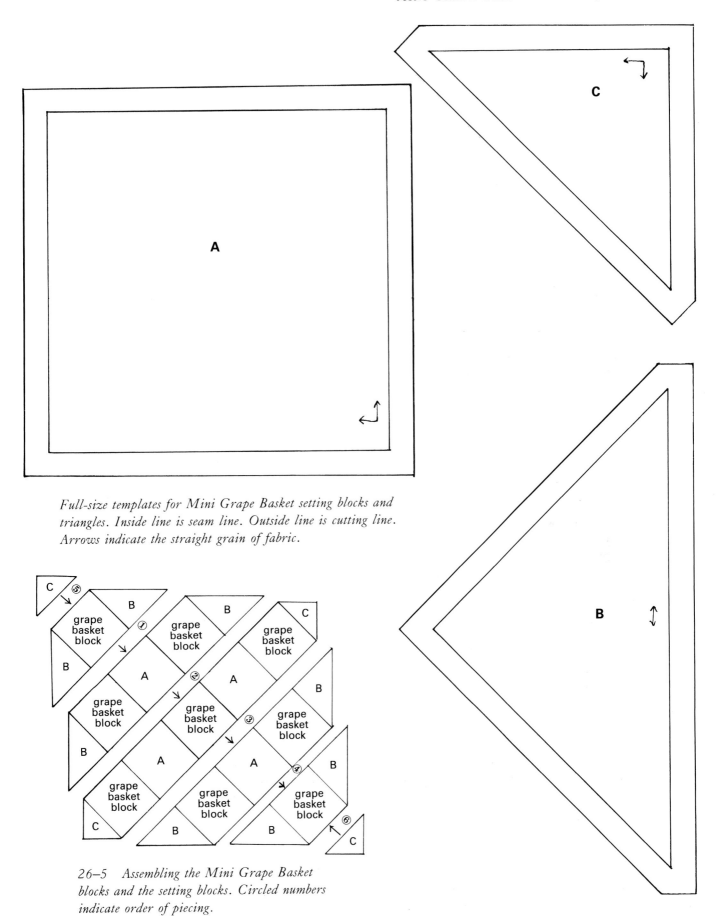

Full-size templates for Mini Grape Basket setting blocks and triangles. Inside line is seam line. Outside line is cutting line. Arrows indicate the straight grain of fabric.

26–5 *Assembling the Mini Grape Basket blocks and the setting blocks. Circled numbers indicate order of piecing.*

27. Nine-Patch Single Irish Chain Doll's Quilt

21″ × 27″ (53.3 cm × 68.6 cm)

The Nine-Patch quilt block has almost endless design possibilities. Because it is very simple to construct, it is an excellent quilt on which to learn. It is especially nice for a young quiltmaker. The design is used here for a doll's quilt in a setting arrangement known as the Single Irish Chain. The simplicity of construction and the finished project make it a good choice for a child's first quilt.

The color combination shown is a replica of a full-sized Amish quilt made in the 1920s. Fabrics and colors shown are similar to the original. The peach and tan are polished cotton or cotton sateen, the black used here was matte black. (All were sateen in the original.) If you're uncertain about the choice of black for a doll's quilt because you think black may be too depressing, ask yourself which is more depressing—a black doll's quilt or a quilt showing soil after only a few hours of play?

Our model is quilted with crosses in the small peach squares and with hearts and flowers in the large black squares. The borders are quilted with cable motifs, which carry across to the corner squares. These motifs may be found in the quilting motifs section at the back of the book.

I suggest chain piecing to speed up your work on the Nine-Patch blocks. See Project 8 (Double Irish Chain Quilt) for chain-piecing instructions. Alternatively, you may want to try your hand at the strip-method speed piecing technique, for which instructions are given below.

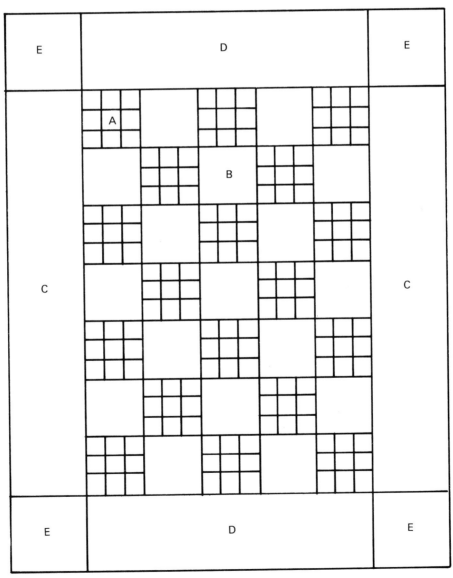

Diagram of finished Nine-Patch Single Irish Chain Doll's Quilt.

YARDAGE

PIECE	COLOR	AMOUNT
A,B,C,D	1 (Black)	⅝ yard
A	2 (Pink)	⅜ yard
A (center of nine-patch block); E, binding	3 (Tan)	¼ yard
Backing	Your choice	¾ yard
Batting	—	24" × 30"

CUTTING: TRADITIONAL METHOD

PIECE	COLOR	QUANTITY	SIZE
A	1 (Black)	72	Template A
A	2 (Pink)	72	Template A
A	3 (Tan)	18	Template A
B	1 (Black)	17	Template B
C	1 (Black)	2	4½" × 21½"
D	1 (Black)	2	4½" × 15½"
E	3 (Tan)	4	4½" × 4½"

CONSTRUCTION: TRADITIONAL METHOD

All construction is done with seam allowances of ¼". First you will make the Nine-Patch blocks, of which a total of 18 are needed.

1. Take four "A" squares in Color 1 (black); we will call these A1. Take four "A" squares in Color 2 (A2). Take one "A" square in Color 3 (A3). Following Figure 27–1 for the color scheme, lay out the pieces as shown. Seam them together into three rectangles of three pieces each. You can use chain piecing to speed up the process (see instructions in Project 8, Double Irish Chain Quilt).

2. Take the three rectangles you created in Step 1. Seam them together into a Nine-Patch block (see Figure 27–2). You now have completed one basic unit of the quilt.

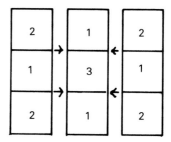

27–1   Seam A squares into three columns, then seam columns together to form a nine-patch unit.

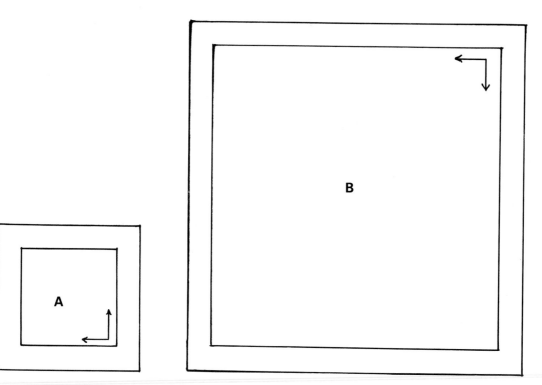

Full-size templates for Single Irish Chain Doll's Quilt. Inner line is seam line; outer line is cutting line. Arrows indicate the straight grain of fabric.

3. Repeat Steps 1 and 2 seventeen more times to make a total of 18 Nine-Patch blocks.

4. Take two B squares of Color 1 (black) and three of the pieced 9-patch blocks you created in steps 1 through 3. Following Figure 27–3, lay out the blocks in a row. Seam the five blocks together in a row, alternating them as shown in Figure 27–3, beginning and ending with a Nine-Patch block. We will call the row we created Unit I.

5. Repeat Step 4 three more times. The four Unit I rows made will be used for rows 1, 3, 5, and 7 of the quilt (see the diagram of the finished quilt). Set these aside for now.

6. Take three B squares of Color 1 (black) and two Nine-Patch blocks. Lay out the five squares as shown in Figure 27–4. Seam the five blocks together in a row, alternating solid blocks with Nine-Patch blocks as shown in Figure 27–4, to make Unit II.

7. Repeat Step 6 two more times. The Unit II pieces will be used for rows 2, 4, and 6 of the quilt top.

8. Consulting the diagram of the finished quilt, lay out the seven rows of the central design, which you made in steps 4 through 7. Be sure that the Unit I rows alternate with the Unit II rows. Seam the seven rows together horizontally, starting with rows 1 and 2 and working your way down. You have now completed the central design.

9. To attach the borders, first take two C borders. Attach them to the long sides of the central panel made in Step 8. See the diagram of the finished quilt for reference.

10. Take the two D borders and four E squares. Seam an E square to each short end of each D border piece to create two E–D–E border units.

11. Take the two E–D–E border units you created in Step 10 and attach one to the top and one to the bottom of the unit you created in Step 9. You have now completed the quilt top. Press the quilt top.

12. To finish the project, see quilting and binding instructions at the back of the book.

CUTTING: ALTERNATE, SPEED-PIECING STRIP METHOD

For the alternate, speed-piecing strip method, cut the strips across the grain of the fabric, from selvage to selvage (see Figure 27–5). Instead of cutting individual squares for piecing, you will create strips first and make your blocks out of them. This will save the time that otherwise would have been needed to sew 54 rectangles of three squares each, as is done in the traditional method.

PIECE	COLOR	QUANTITY	SIZE
For A squares	1 (Black)	4	1½″ × 45″
For A squares	2 (Pink)	4	1½″ × 45″
For A squares	3 (Tan)	1	1½″ × 45″
For B squares	1 (Black)	2	3½″ × 45″
C	1 (Black)	2	4½″ × 21½″
D	1 (Black)	2	4½″ × 15½″
E	3 (Tan)	4	4½″ × 4½″

27–2   The completed nine-patch block.

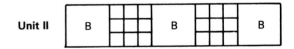

27–3   Seam nine-patch to solid blocks as shown, to make Unit I. This is used for rows 1, 3, 5, and 7 of the quilt.

27–4   Seam nine-patch to solid blocks as shown to make Unit II. This is used for rows 2, 4, and 6 of the quilt.

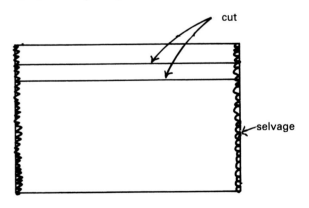

27–5   For speed piecing method, cut strips from selvage to selvage.

ALTERNATE SPEED METHOD OF CONSTRUCTION

1. All construction is done with ¼" seam allowance. First make two bands of 3 strips each. Take two strips of size 1½" × 45" of Color 2 and one strip 1½" × 45" of Color 1. Sew them together along their long sides so that Color 1 is in the middle, to form Band I (Figure 27–6).

2. Take two strips 1½" × 45" of Color 1 and one strip 1½" × 45" of Color 3. Sew them together along their long sides so that Color 3 is in the middle, to form Band II (Figure 27–7). Press both bands, keeping the seam allowance on the side of the dark color.

3. Using your gridded ruler, take Band I and check its short edge for squareness, to be sure it is perpendicular to the long edge, that is, it makes a square corner like the corner of your right triangle. If it isn't perpendicular, straighten it, by cutting off the part that extends over the square line with your rotary cutter.

4. Now that Band I is squared up, make thirty-six 1½"-wide bars by slicing across the three stripes of Band I with your rotary cutter. We will call these bars "bar I," since they came from Band I (see Figure 27–8, left). Put these bars aside for the moment.

5. Take Band II, which you created in Step 2. Straighten the short edge as you did in Step 3. Then make eighteen 1½"-wide bars by slicing across the three stripes of Band II. We will call each "bar II" as they came from Band II.

6. Now take two of bar I and one of bar II. As shown in Figure 27–9, join them together to make a Nine-Patch unit. Be sure to observe your ¼" seam allowances.

7. Repeat Step 6 until you have made a total of 18 Nine-Patch units.

8. Take one of the 3½" × 45" strips you made of Color 1 (black, in our model). With your rotary cutter, make twelve 3½"-wide squares by slicing across the strip. Make five 3½"-wide squares from the second 3½" × 45" strip of Color 1. This will give you the total of 17 B blocks you need for piecing the quilt top.

9. From here on, you can follow the construction steps given under Construction: Traditional Method, above. Begin at Step 4 to join the Nine-Patch squares with solid squares.

Color 2
Color 1
Color 2

27–6 Color arrangement for Band I.

Color 1
Color 3
Color 1

27–7 Color arrangement for Band II.

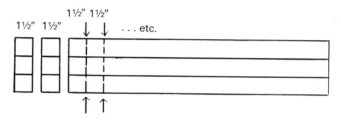

27–8 Cut bars by slicing across bands with rotary cutter.

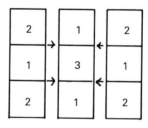

Bar I+   Bar II+   Bar I

27–9 Seam three bars together to make a nine-patch unit. Arabic numbers indicate colors.

28. Star of Bethlehem Quilt

51″ × 51″ (129.5 cm × 129.5 cm)

The Star of Bethlehem is a favorite of Amish quiltmakers, perhaps because it makes such a striking statement. It looks more complicated than it really is. Relatively small amounts of each color are needed to make the star. I know few Amish quiltmakers who have not used this design. It is even more popular generally than the Amish Diamond and Amish Bars. Give it a try.

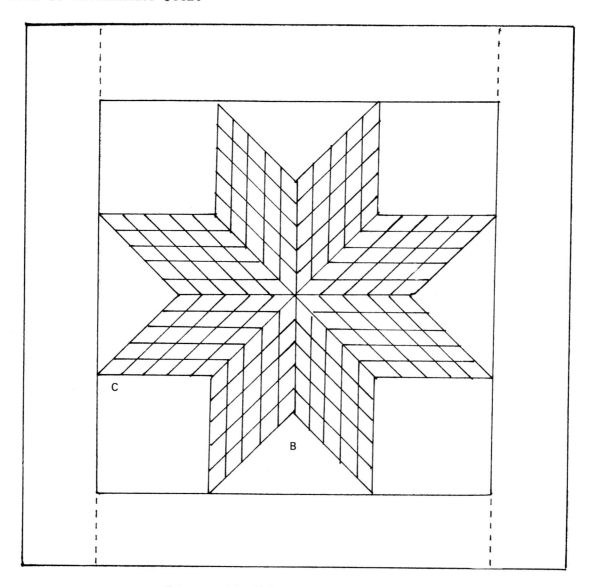

Diagram of finished Star of Bethlehem Quilt.

YARDAGE

PIECE	COLOR	QUANTITY
Star pattern of quilt and optional multicolored border	1 (Teal blue)*	½ yard
	2 (Rose)	½ yard
	3 (Light blue)	½ yard
	4 (Red)	½ yard
	5 (Royal blue)	½ yard
B and C (setting triangles and squares) and border	6 (Black in model)	1½ yards
Backing	6 (Black in model)	54″ × 54″
Batting	—	54″ × 54″

* Colors in parentheses give choices used in the model. You can choose any colors you wish, however.

The instructions here are for quick strip piecing. A rotary cutter, cutting board, and gridded ruler are recommended. You will also need a 10" 45° right triangle. The swag feather border motif may be found in the section on quilting motifs at the back of the book, along with other designs suitable for quilting the large squares and triangles.

The Star of Bethlehem is made up of 8 large pieced diamonds. You will make strips that are then sewn together into strip groups of five colors. The groups will be cut into bands and reassembled to complete the diamond sections of your star. When sewing it will be critical to maintain your ¼" seam allowances.

You can do color sketches on copies of Figure 28–4 to visualize one diamond-shaped unit of the star and try out potential color combinations. The color designated "Color 1" will be the center of the star (it is teal in our model). Colors 2 through 5 will form radiating rounds of the star. The colors repeat in the same order to the outer parts of the star. Even after you have chosen 5 colors, there are many color combinations possible for your quilt, depending on your choice of color order. Choose the colors 1, 2, 3, 4 and 5 you want, after studying Figure 28–4 and the color photograph. It will be helpful if you cut a swatch of each color of material and label it 1, 2, 3, 4, or 5, and set it aside for reference.

CUTTING

1. From each of your five star-design colors (colors 1 through 5), cut five strips, each of which is 2¼" × 45". Cut across the straight grain of the fabric from selvage to selvage. These strips will be used to make the star design. (The optional border is made from the remaining sewn diamond strips).

2. The setting squares, triangles, and borders will be cut later.

3. An optional multicolored border inset (see color photograph) also may be cut later (see Optional Border Inset section, below).

CONSTRUCTION

Creating the Strip Groups

1. Baste and sew the strips together in groups of 5 to form Strip Groups A, B, C, D, and E, as shown in Figure 28–1, and as listed below. Be very careful to maintain accurate ¼" seam allowances.

   Group A: Sew strips in the color order 1–2–3–4–5; press all seams toward Color 5.

   Group B is pieced in color order 2–3–4–5–1; press seam allowances toward Color 2.

   Group C is pieced in order 3–4–5–1–2; press seams toward Color 2.

   Group D is pieced in order 4–5–1–2–3; press seams toward Color 4.

   Group E is pieced in order 5–1–2–3–4; press seams toward Color 4.

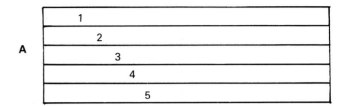

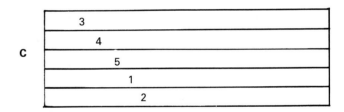

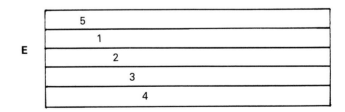

28–1 Assemble 5 groups of 5 strips each as shown in A through E. Numbers refer to colors.

2. Press each strip group from the reverse side first; then turn your work over and press it from the right side also, to avoid leaving any hidden tucks. Pressing seam allowances as indicated makes matching the seams easier and cuts down on the bulk under the seam.

Cutting the Strip Groups Into Bands

The next step is to slice across the strip groups to create 5-colored bands of small diamonds, which will later be assembled into large diamonds. An example of one band (cut from Group A) is shown in Figure 28–2.

3. Take Strip Group A. Be sure it is laid out on your cutting board with Color 1 at the top. Carefully align the base of your 45° right triangle with the long, bottom edge of Strip Group A. Consult Figure 28–3. You will have some waste at the lower left corner, because in order to make a full band of all 5 colors, you need to move your triangle in from the left edge 10″ to make the first cut. Mark the line with a fabric marker and cut along the line with your rotary cutter, being careful to maintain your 45° angle.

4. Using your gridded ruler and rotary cutter, carefully measure and cut 2¼″-wide slices of Strip Group A. See Figure 28–3 for reference. Still using your triangle, make a second cut, also at 45° to the bottom line, as the first cut was. You have now cut out one Band A unit.

5. Continue measuring and cutting 2¼″-wide units, until you have cut a total of eight Band A units. Label each one at the top with a small piece of paper or masking tape so they don't get mixed up with the other units.

6. Repeat Steps 3 through 5 with strip groups B, C, D, and E, cutting 8 bands from each one.

Diamond Construction

Reminder: Be very sure to keep your ¼″ seam allowances precisely.

7. Following Figure 28–4 as a guide, take a Band A unit and a Band B unit. Pin them together with right sides facing, being sure colors are positioned as in Figure 28–4. When pinned, the band units will not totally overlap each other (Figure 28–5). Baste and sew them together. The seam lines will create an X as they intersect.

8. Repeat Step 7 until you have created seven more Band A/Band B units, one for each big diamond that makes up the star pattern.

9. To each of the Band A/Band B units created in steps 7 and 8, pin, baste, and sew a Band C next to Band B, as shown in Figure 28–4.

10. To each Band A/Band B/Band C unit you made in Step 9, sew a Band D unit as shown in Figure 28–4.

11. To each Band A/Band B/Band C/Band D unit you made in Step 10, add a Band E unit as shown in Figure 28–4. This completes all eight diamonds needed to make the star design. The center point will be Color 1.

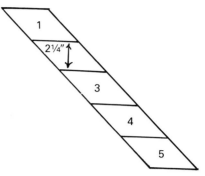

28–2   *Example of a band that will be pieced into the large diamond. Not all bands have same color order.*

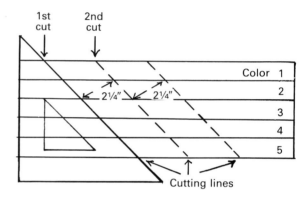

28–3   *Cutting strip group A into 8 bands, using 45° triangle.*

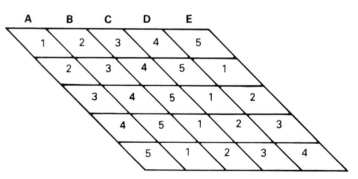

28–4   *Order of attaching band units to form a large diamond. Numbers indicate colors. Seam lines form an X where they meet.*

Star Construction

12. Study Figure 28–6. You will see that the large diamonds meet at the center in Color 1.

13. Take two of the large diamonds and pin, baste, and seam the sections together along the bands that have colors in order 1–2–3–4–5 (Band A), placing Color 1 of the first large diamond next to Color 1 of the second large diamond, Color 2 with Color 2, etc., to make the jagged circles that form the pattern (see color figure). Start your seams ¼" in from the material's edge and stop ¼" from the material's edge, working from the center of the star (Color 1) outward. It will make the insetting of the background squares and triangles easier when you come to them later.

14. Take a third large diamond and pin, baste, and sew it in place on the unit you created in Step 13, attaching Color 1 to Color 1, and the other colors to their same colors, as you did for the first two large diamonds. Then attach a fourth large diamond in the same way (see Figure 28–6). You now have completed half of the star pattern. Set this half aside.

15. Repeat steps 13 and 14 to create the second half of the star pattern out of the remaining 4 large diamonds.

16. To join the two halves of the star, pin the two halves together starting from the center of the star and pinning outward in each direction. Check to be sure that they are aligned correctly and baste and sew in place. There should not be any gap between the parts.

Corners and Triangles

17. Check the size of the squares (C) you will need to fill in the corners of the star pattern (see Figure 28–7 for placement of squares). Your star should require about 12½" or 13" squares (finished size; cut ½" larger squares to include their seam allowances). However, as your star pattern may have ended up being slightly larger or smaller after it was sewn, we suggest that you cut a paper or cardboard outline of your square, based on the space you have in the corner of your star pattern when you lay it out flat; then add ¼" on each side for a seam allowance and make a cardboard template. Cut out 4 setting squares from your background material (Color 6), using the square template; be sure the right angles are on the grain line of the fabric. This will help prevent stretching along the outer sides of your quilt top. Don't set in the squares yet, however.

18. You can use the cardboard template of the square that you made in Step 17 to create a pattern for the four B triangles needed to set the star design. Cut the square pattern template in half on the diagonal, add ¼" seam allowances to each of the three sides of one cardboard triangle, and cut a new cardboard template. Then cut out the four setting triangles from the background material (Color 6), using the new cardboard template, with the straight grain of fabric on the long edge of the triangle (which will be the outer edge of the star block).

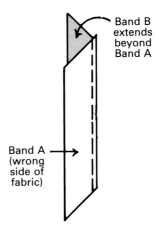

28–5 When two band units are pinned for stitching, they will not totally overlap each other.

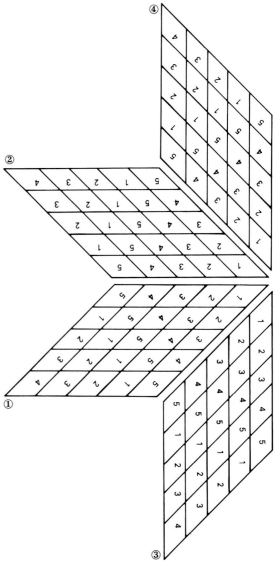

28–6 Assemble 4 large diamonds to make half of the star pattern. Circled numbers refer to the order of assembling.

19. Take your four setting triangles. Insert the triangles along the middles of the four sides of the star (see Figure 28–7), by pinning and basting them in place, matching the sides to the sides of each adjacent diamond, and then sewing them from the inner point outward on one triangle side and repeating the process on the other triangle side.

20. After you have set in all four triangles, you can complete the central design block by setting in the squares. Pin and baste them in place in the corners, as shown in Figure 28–7. Stitch from the right angle of each star outward to attach the square. Go back to the right angle where the square joins the star to stitch the second side of each square.

Final Borders*

21. We suggest borders of about 5″ width to finish your quilt. The border quilt design shown in the model fits on a 5″ wide border nicely. Cut strips of 5½″ × about 48″ for the top and bottom border and 5½″ × about 58″ for the side borders. The exact length may be checked across the center of the quilt. Piece borders if necessary.

22. Mark the middle of the border length of each side and align it with the middle of the unit you created by joining the star pattern and the squares and triangles. Pin, baste, and sew the top and bottom borders in place.

23. Then pin the side border units to the unit you created in Step 22, matching the middle of the design with the middle of the border length and working outward in both directions. Try not to stretch the border pieces. Do not mitre the corners—it's not Amish.

Optional Border Inset

24. The thin, striped border shown in the color photograph is stitched in place as a strip. The bands that form the optional border are cut from leftover strip groups A, B, C, D, and E, which were used to make the star. As the recommended width of the optional border is 1″, you need to cut bands that are 1½″ wide. Cut them on a 45° angle as you did earlier when you created the bands to make the star pattern (steps 3 through 6), only these are narrower. You need to cut about 16 bands, of any strip groups you choose.

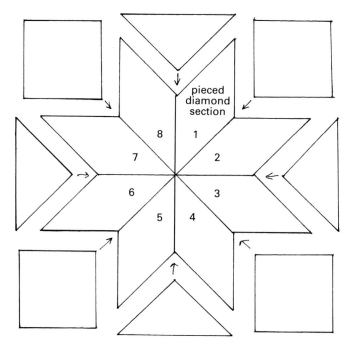

28–7 Attach the setting triangles and squares around the star pattern.

25. Join 4 bands end to end for each side of the border inset, measuring the perimeter of the large pieced square to see exactly how long you need to make the border inset, and adding on ½″ to each border for seam allowances. The border units probably will be about 48″ long each. As they are cut on the bias, the individual bars are very stretchy, so be careful not to pull and stretch them while you are attaching them to the borders of the quilt top.

26. Attach the border insets to the top and bottom and then to the right and left sides of the center panel. To attach the outer borders, see steps 21–23 above.

27. To prepare to quilt, first transfer the designs to your quilt top, using the swag feather border given in the template section at the back of the book if you wish to. You can transfer the design using a lightbox or light table. Tape a dark copy of the pattern onto the lightbox and then draw the pattern onto the quilt top with dressmaker's chalk or a fabric marker. Another method is to make a cardboard or plastic template of the design and trace around it on the quilt top. See the general quilting and binding instructions at the back of the book to finish the project.

---

* If you intend to make the optional striped borders, see steps 24–26 before making the final borders.

29. Rainbow Log Cabin Quilt

68" × 76" (172.7 cm × 193 cm)

The Log Cabin design in the photograph is of the variety known as Barn Raising. There is almost no wasted fabric from yardage cut into strips for Log Cabin piecing. The Amish-style Log Cabin block cleverly allows for reduced consumption of very light fabrics.

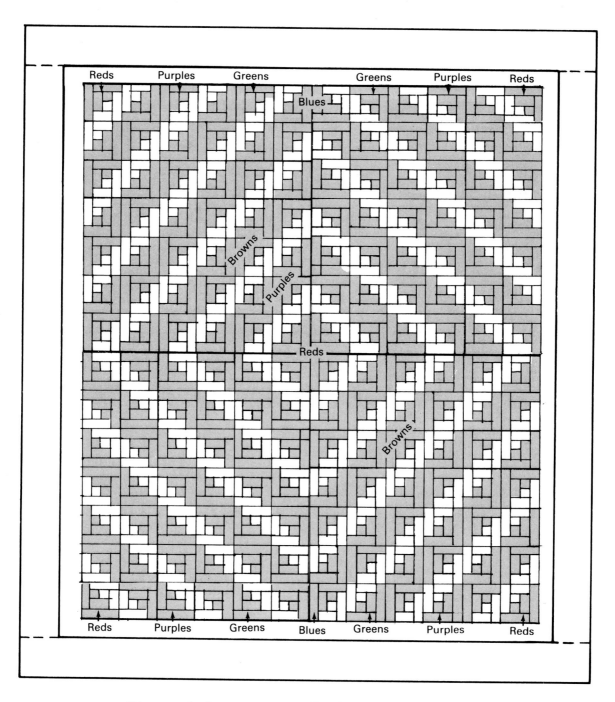

Diagram of color arrangement in Rainbow Log Cabin Quilt.

While it is not immediately apparent, there is one-third less light fabric used in the Amish block construction than there is in an "English" block. Since the Amish use light colors sparingly in clothing for practical purposes, this design may enable the Amish quiltmaker to complete the quilt from scraps on hand.

For the quilt shown here you will need to make 168 blocks (12 across and 14 down). You can use the template patterns A, B, C, and D provided here or speed-cut strips with a rotary cutter. Cutting instructions are given for both.

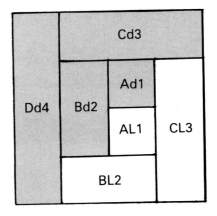

YARDAGE

Each block has a "light" (L) and "dark" (d) side to make up the pattern (Figure 29–1). For the light side (done entirely in light gray in our model), you can use light to medium-light shades of gray, green, blue, tan, or taupe. The total "light" yardage should be approximately 4 yards. It is almost always the case that an Amish quiltmaker doesn't consider yardage for inner and outer borders until they are actually needed. By that time she'll know what colors she wishes to emphasize.

As it isn't frugal to be so cavalier and most of us would prefer not to have seams in wide border areas, border yardages are given in the yardage chart. However, you also may wish to wait until the main design is pieced before you choose colors for the borders.

29–1 Basic Log Cabin block, Amish style. A, B, C, D are template sizes. "d" colors are the dark colors of the block. "L" colors are light colors (gray in the model).

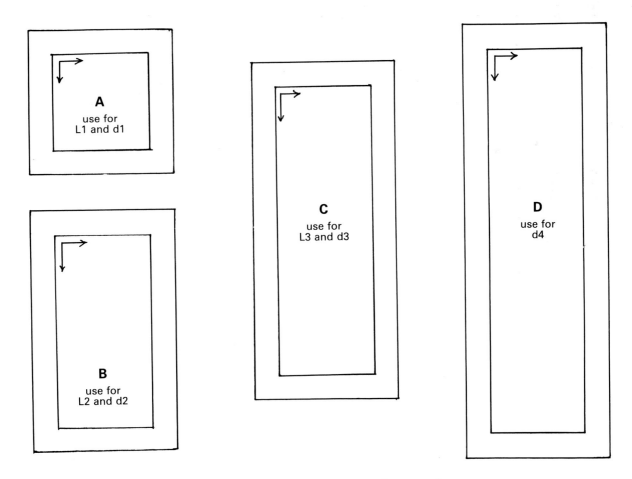

Full-size templates for the Rainbow Log Cabin Quilt. Outer lines are cutting lines. Inner lines are seam lines. Arrows indicate the straight grain of fabric.

Yardage: Either Method

PIECE	COLOR	QUANTITY
	REDS	
"Dark" sides of red blocks	Very dark red, medium dark red, bright red, dusty rose	1/8 yard of each
	PURPLES	
"Dark" sides of purple blocks	Very dark bluish purple, burgundy (very dark wine), periwinkle, light purple	1/4 yard of each
	GREENS	
"Dark" sides of green blocks	Very dark blackish green, dark bluish green, olive green, light olive green	3/8 yard of each
	BLUES	
"Dark" sides of blue blocks	Very dark blue, medium cobalt blue, medium purplish blue, light blue	3/8 yard of each
	BROWNS	
"Dark" sides of brown blocks	Very dark brown, medium reddish brown, yellow ochre (yellowish tan), orange-pink (coral)	1/4 yard of each
"Light" sides of all blocks	Your choice of light to medium light gray, green, blue, tan, taupe, or other light shades (light gray in model)	Total of all colors to equal about 4 yards
Inner border	Your choice (dark blue in model)	3/4 yard
Outer border	Your choice (light gray in model)	2 1/4 yards
Backing	Your choice	4 yards
Batting	—	72" × 80"

* Colors given are those used in the model. You can vary them by using 4 varieties of any five colors for the "dark" colors.

For the pattern shown, you will make the following number of blocks (identified by dark color only): Reds: 8 blocks. Purples: 40 blocks. Greens: 36 blocks. Blues: 48 blocks. Browns: 36 blocks.

CUTTING

Cutting charts are given for both the pieced method (in which each block is cut separately) and speed cutting. Refer to Figure 29–1 to see the position of the dark (d) colors and the light (L) colors in each block.

Cutting: Pieced Method (Using Templates)

PIECE & SIZE*	COLOR**	TOTAL QUANTITY FOR QUILT
	RED BLOCKS	
A, B, C, D (dark side)	Vary colors of pieces among 4 reds	8 of each size
A, B, C (light side)	Vary colors of pieces among "light" colors	8 of each size
	PURPLE BLOCKS	
A, B, C, D (dark side)	Vary colors of pieces among 4 purples	40 of each size
A, B, C (light side)	Vary colors of pieces among "light" colors	40 of each size
	GREEN BLOCKS	
A, B, C, D (dark side)	Vary colors of pieces among 4 greens	36 of each size
A, B, C (light side)	Vary colors of pieces among "light" colors	36 of each size
	BLUE BLOCKS	
A, B, C, D (dark side)	Vary colors of pieces among 4 blues	48 of each size
A, B, C (light side)	Vary colors of pieces among "light" colors	48 of each size
	BROWN BLOCKS	
A, B, C, D (dark side)	Vary colors of pieces among 4 browns	36 of each size
A, B, C (light side)	Vary colors of pieces among "light" colors	36 of each size
	BORDERS†	
Inner borders	Your choice (blue in model)	2 long, 2 short
Outer borders	Your choice (light gray in model)	2 long, 2 short

* For A, B, C, and D use Templates A, B, C and D, respectively.
** Light colors are all gray in model.
†For border cutting see Step 31.

Speed-Cutting Strip Method

Instead of cutting individual rectangles for piecing, create strips first and make pieces out of them. This saves cutting time. Cut 1½″ wide strips across the grain of the fabric from selvage to selvage. The amounts to cut are given in the accompanying tables, "Cutting Guide for Speed Cutting Strip Method." The "dark" sides of the blocks are given first. If you want to vary the colors of the blocks so that not all "A" squares in the blue blocks, for example, are light blue, you can cut some strips of the light blue color and some of another blue; however, the total number of A blocks of some color of blue is still 48.

Cutting for Speed Cutting Strip Method: Dark Sides

PIECE*	STRIP SIZE	NUMBER OF STRIPS TO CUT	LENGTH OF PIECES TO CUT	QUANTITY OF PIECES FROM STRIPS
		RED BLOCKS		
d1	1½″ × 15″	1	1½″	8
d2	1½″ × 20″	1	2½″	8
d3	1½″ × 28″	1	3½″	8
d4	1½″ × 36″	1	4½″	8
		PURPLE BLOCKS		
d1	1½″ × 45″	1	1½″	40
	1½″ × 15″	1		
d2	1½″ × 45″	2	2½″	40
	1½″ × 10″	1		
d3	1½″ × 45″	3	3½″	40
	1½″ × 15″	1		
d4	1½″ × 45″	4	4½″	40
		GREEN BLOCKS		
d1	1½″ × 45″	1	1½″	36
	1½″ × 10″	1		
d2	1½″ × 45″	2	2½″	36
d3	1½″ × 45″	3	3½″	36
d4	1½″ × 45″	3	4½″	36
	1½″ × 30″	1		
		BLUE BLOCKS		
d1	1½″ × 45″	1	1½″	48
	1½″ × 30″	1		
d2	1½″ × 45″	2	2½″	48
	1½″ × 30″	1		
d3	1½″ × 45″	4	3½″	48
d4	1½″ × 45″	3	4½″	48
	1½″ × 38″	1		
		BROWN BLOCKS		
d1	1½″ × 45″	1	1½″	36
	1½″ × 10″	1		
d2	1½″ × 45″	2	2½″	36
d3	1½″ × 45″	3	3½″	36
d4	1½″ × 45″	3	4½″	36
	1½″ × 30″	1		

* Colors may be varied as you choose within the color group so that each size of piece is not always the same color.

The following chart gives the number and size of strips needed for the light (L) parts of all blocks (light gray in the model).

Cutting for Speed Strip Method: Light Sides

COLOR	STRIP SIZE	NUMBER OF STRIPS	WIDTH OF PIECES TO CUT	QUANTITY OF PIECES
L1	1½″ × 45″	6	1½″	168
L2	1½″ × 45″	10	2½″	168
L3	1½″ × 45″	14	3½″	168

Slice across the strips with a rotary cutter to create individual pieces. First square up the corners of the strips, measuring them on a ruled board or with a right-angle triangle, and cutting off the excess that isn't square with your rotary cutter. (See Figure 29–2 for reference in cutting pieces.)

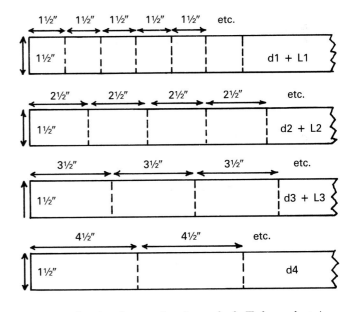

29–2 Cutting for speed strip method. Take each strip and slice across it with a rotary cutter to make pieces of widths indicated.

CONSTRUCTION

All construction is done with a seam allowance of ¼″. The 168 blocks are pieced in exactly the same way, using the range of the four dark shades (d1, d2, d3, and d4) of the base color for that particular square (red, green, purple, brown, or blue in the model). In our model, all the light (L) pieces are light gray; however, as you may have chosen other light colors, we will refer to these as L1, L2, L3 (see Figure 29–1).

Piecing the Blocks (Figure 29-3)

1. To piece one block, take one each of the 4 sizes of rectangle (A, B, C, and D) in one dark base color and one each of the three light rectangles A, B, and C (gray in the model). Take an A square of color d1 (Ad1) and an A square of color L1 (AL1). Attach them on one side.

2. Attach a B rectangle in color d2 of your base color (Bd2) to the long side of the unit made in Step 1 (see Figure 29-3).

3. Attach a B rectangle of the light color L2 (BL2) to the unit made in Step 2.

4. Attach a C rectangle of the light color L3 (CL3) to the unit made in Step 3.

5. Attach a C rectangle in color d3 of your base color (Cd3) to the unit made in Step 4.

6. Attach a D rectangle of base color d4 (Dd4) to the unit made in Step 5. This completes one block.

7. Repeat steps 1 through 6 to make each of the remaining 167 blocks for the quilt top. When you have completed them, press the squares, with the seam allowances to the dark sides.

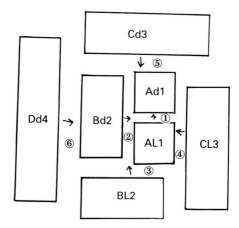

29–3 *Order of piecing of single block. Circled numbers indicate order of piecing. d1, d2, d3, d4, and L1, L2, and L3 indicate colors. A, B, C and D are template sizes.*

Assembling the Blocks

8. As the quilt top is large, assemble quarters of it individually and then join the quarters together. The upper left and lower right quarters are assembled in exactly the same way. Study the color photo for guidance.

Upper Left Quarter and Lower Right Quarter (Figure 29-4)

9. The upper left quarter of the quilt top (without borders) is made up of 7 rows of 6 squares each. Seam the blocks together in order for each row (illustrated in Figure 29–4). Assemble the blocks one row at a time and set each row aside as it is finished. Be sure to match the "dark" sides as indicated, to keep the pattern. You might label each row with a piece of masking tape so that you can easily tell which is which later.

10. Seam the blocks of Row 1 together in the following order from left to right:
red–purple–purple–green–green–blue.

11. For Row 2 seam the blocks together in the order:
purple–purple–green–green–blue–blue.

12. For Row 3 seam the blocks together in the order:
purple–green–green–blue–blue–brown.

13. For Row 4 seam the blocks together in the order:
green–green–blue–blue–brown–brown.

14. For Row 5 seam the blocks together in the order:
green–blue–blue–brown–brown–purple.

15. For Row 6 seam the blocks together in the order:
blue–blue–brown–brown–purple–purple.

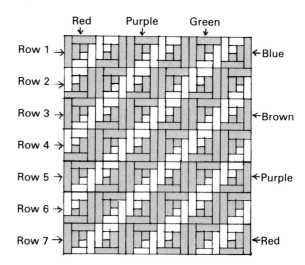

29–4 *Assembly order of upper left quarter and lower right quarter.*

16. For Row 7 seam the blocks together in the order:
blue–brown–brown–purple–purple–red.

17. Lay out the rows you just made for the upper left quarter of the design and compare the result with Figure 29–4 to be sure the rows are placed and oriented correctly.

18. Sew the rows together in order, matching seam lines, until you have finished the whole quarter. Press it.

19. Repeat Steps 9 through 18 to make the lower right quarter, which is exactly the same as the upper left quarter; later it is turned upside down when the quarters are assembled.

The Upper Right Quarter and Lower Left Quarter (Figure 29–5)

20. See Figure 29–5 for layout of rows and blocks in the upper right quarter, which is made of 7 rows of 6 blocks each. Assemble the blocks one row at a time, matching dark sides of the blocks to make the pattern. Label and set aside each row as you make it.

21. For Row 1 of the upper right quarter, seam the blocks together in the order: blue–green–green–purple–purple–red.

22. For Row 2 seam the blocks together in the order: blue–blue–green–green–purple–purple.

23. For Row 3, seam the blocks in the order: brown–blue–blue–green–green–purple.

24. For Row 4 seam the blocks together in the order: brown–brown–blue–blue–green–green.

25. For Row 5 seam the blocks together in the order: purple–brown–brown–blue–blue–green.

26. For Row 6 seam the blocks together in the order: purple–purple–brown–brown–green–green.

27. For Row 7 seam blocks in the order: red–purple–purple–brown–brown–blue.

28. Lay out the rows you just made for the upper right quarter and compare with Figure 29–5 to be sure they are placed and oriented correctly.

29. Sew the rows together in order until you have finished the whole upper right quarter. Press it.

30. Repeat steps 20 through 29 to create the lower left quarter, which is the same as the upper right quarter (it will be turned upside down in assembly). Label it to avoid confusion later.

Assembling the Quarters

31. Lay out all 4 quarters. Compare them with the diagram of color arrangement for the whole quilt to be sure that they are all oriented correctly. Matching seamlines and edges, sew the quarters together. This completes the Rainbow Log Cabin part of the top.

Borders and Finishing the Quilt Top

32. *Cutting and attaching inner borders.* All borders are cut on straight grain of fabric. Measure across the top and sides of the Rainbow Log Cabin panel. It should be about 48″ × 56″. To make the inner borders, you need to cut two short strips for the top and bottom and two long strips for the sides. Make the long strips the length of the central panel, plus ½″ for the seam allowances (about 56.5″) × 2½″ wide. Make the two short, inner border strips about 52.5″ (this includes ½″ for seam allowances) × 2½″. Piece fabric if necessary.

33. Take the two long inner border pieces and sew one to each side of the center Rainbow Log Cabin panel. Take the two short inner border strips and sew one across the top and one along the bottom of the center Rainbow Log Cabin panel.

34. *Cutting and attaching outer border strips.* Measure your quilt along the side, including the inner borders you just attached. It should be about 60.5″. Cut two outer border sides (long) strips the length of the side plus ½″ × 7½″. On the sides of the panel, attach the long outer border strips to the inner borders. Measure the quilt across the width, including the inner borders and side outer borders, at the top. It should be about 68″. Cut two outer border short strips 7½″ × the width of the quilt top plus ½″. Attach the outer border short strips to the top and bottom of the quilted panel you created thus far. This completes the quilt top.

35. To complete the project, see instructions on quilting and binding at the back of the book.

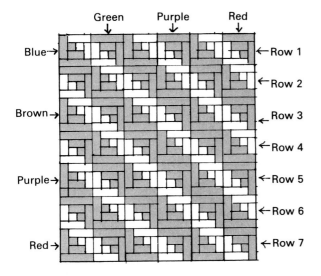

29–5 Assembly order of upper right quarter and lower left quarter.

30. Amish Doll Sara

16″ (40.6 cm) tall

For decades, conservative Amish households have provided dolls with no faces for their children. The absence of the face and hair reflect the reluctance to create an image. I think it's wonderful! The hardest part of any doll is making the face and hair, and now you're free of that task. Your child can use the gift of imagination to create the doll's expressions. You may want to cut your pattern pieces from interfacing rather than from paper, because interfacing lasts longer. This is a project that you probably will want to repeat.

YARDAGE AND OTHER SUPPLIES

PART	AMOUNT AND COLORS
Doll's body	¾ yard muslin, weavers' cloth or broadcloth in white or ivory
	1 lb. polyester fiberfill stuffing ¾ yard featherweight interfacing for making pattern (optional) Four white buttons, about ½" diameter
Dress	½ yard solid-colored broadcloth of a dark to medium shade
Apron	⅜ yard solid-colored broadcloth, voile, batiste, or black organdy (Dress and apron are usually made of different colors.)
Bonnet	½ yard black broadcloth
	2⅝" × 9" bonnet board or stiff but flexible cardboard (or template plastic)
	¾ yard of ¼" black ribbon, either satin or grosgrain, cut into two pieces
	25" light-gauge wire (#20)
Threads	Black and colors to match dress and apron fabrics
Needle	A 3" to 5" sculpting needle to attach the limbs

CUTTING

Dress

1. With fabric folded lengthwise to make a rectangle that is 9" × 45", place pattern pieces A, B, and C in place and cut them out; ¼" seam allowance is included.

2. Then open out the dress fabric after cutting out A, B, and C, and measure and cut one piece 8½" × 19" for the skirt part of the dress; cut one piece 1" × 12" at an angle to the grain line (on the bias) for the neck facing.

Apron

1. Place pattern piece D on the folded fabric, positioning the pattern on the fold, as indicated. Extend length of apron 1½" beyond pattern's end. Pin pattern to fabric and cut out apron.

2. In addition, cut one piece of material on the bias that is ¾" × 8½". This will be the facing of the apron neck.

Doll's Body and Head

1. With fabric for the doll's body folded, lay out and trace pieces J, E and F. You must lift pieces F and E and turn the pattern pieces to the opposite side and trace them a second time to create the second side of the arm and second side of the leg.

2. After you have traced and cut J, E, and F, open out the remainder of the material and trace and cut one each of pieces G, H, I, and K.

CONSTRUCTION

Pieces are designed with ¼" seam allowances.

Dress Construction

1. Turn up ¼" of lower edge of sleeve toward the right side of the fabric and roll ¾" hem up on the right side of each sleeve. This makes a false cuff and also hems the sleeve. Topstitch the hem to the sleeve at the upper edge of the ¾" hem to hold it in place.

2. Take Piece B (bodice front) and both of Piece A (bodice back). With right sides of material together, pin or baste the bodice back sections A to the bodice front B at the shoulders, matching numbers and seam lines, and stitch shoulder from #1 to #2 on pattern.

3. Pin and baste the sleeve in place in the bodice, with right sides of the material facing each other, and the center of the sleeve at the top of the armhole. Sew the sleeve into the armhole along the armhole seam line. Repeat for the second sleeve.

4. Turn the dress bodice right side out.

5. Take the dress neck facing (1" × 12"). Turn over ¼" hem on one long side of the facing, so that the ¼" hem is on the wrong side of the fabric.

6. With the right side of the facing touching the right side of the dress, pin and baste the unhemmed long side of the facing to the neck opening, with the short ends of the facing aligned with the openings in the dress bodice back. Sew the facing to the neck opening along the side you just pinned and basted. If necessary, trim the seam allowance to within ⅛" of seamline to avoid bunching. Turn the facing to the inside (wrong side) of the dress, and slipstitch the facing in place.

7. At the bodice back, turn under ⅛" along the bodice back opening and stitch it down on both sides of the bodice back. Then turn under another ½" to be the back center facing and stitch it in place on both sides of the bodice back opening.

8. Matching #9 with #9 and #10 with #10 on the sleeve, pin the sleeve edges together with right sides facing each other. Pin the sides of the bodice front to the bodice back, matching #3 on the front to #3 on the back and #4 on the front to #4 on the back of the bodice. Seam the side and sleeve seams as one continuous line of stitching, starting from the lower seam of the bodice and working towards the outer edge of the sleeve.

9. Take the skirt rectangle (8½" × 19"). Run two rows of basting stitches along the 19" side of the rectangle, ⅛" in (towards the cutting line) from the seamline. Pull the basting threads to gather the skirt, distribute the gathers evenly, and pin the skirt to the bodice at the waistline with right sides of material facing each other, matching the opening of the bodice back to the opening of the skirt back. Baste and sew the skirt to the waist of the bodice.

10. Close up the back of the skirt seam from the lower part to within 1½" of the waistline. Turn under ¼" of the back skirt opening and pin it to the wrong side of the material. Then pin under another ¼" on both sides for a back facing. Attach one-half of a small snap at the top of each side of the neck opening to hold the dress closed.

11. Hem the lower edge of the skirt by hand or by machine.

Doll's Body Construction

Arms and Legs

1. Take the E arm pieces. Stitch two E pieces together, matching #1 with #1 on each piece, #2 with #2, and so on up to #8, leaving an opening for stuffing, as indicated on the pattern piece. Trim curved areas of seams to within ⅛" of seamline to ease curve lines.

2. Repeat Step 1 to make the second arm.

3. Turn the arm units right side out. Take your polyester fiberfill or whatever material you are using for stuffing. Make small tufts of stuffing and push the stuffing into the arm units until they are stuffed firmly.

4. Tuck the seam allowances of the stuffing holes on the arms inside and overcast the openings closed by hand. Set the arms aside for now.

5. Take two F leg pieces. With right sides of material together, stitch the two F pieces together, starting at #9, sewing to #10, and working around to #16, matching #9 of one F piece to the #9 of the second F piece, and matching all the other numbers to their same numbers. Leave an opening for stuffing. Trim the seam allowances to facilitate turning of piece, as was done with the arms. Turn the leg unit right side out.

6. Take the two remaining leg pieces. Proceed as in Step 5.

7. Take the two leg units. Proceeding as for the arms in steps 3 and 4, stuff the legs and close up the stuffing openings by overcast stitching them closed by hand.

Head

1. Pin Piece I (the left side of the back of the doll's head) to H (the center of the back of the doll's head), starting at the side of the neck edge and matching #1 on H to #1 on I, #3 on H to #3 on I, and #2 on H to #2 on I. Trim curves to within ⅛" of seamline to ease fabric parts together, if necessary. Machine stitch from #1 to #2.

2. Take Piece K and, with right side of material facing right side of material of Piece H, pin, baste, and seam K to H starting at the neck edge and matching #6 to #6, #5 to #5, and #4 to #4 (Fig. 30–1). You now have made a 3-piece back-of-head unit.

3. Take G, the front of the doll's head. On the wrong side of the material, stitch the darts closed, working from the neck edge to the point of the dart.

4. With right sides of material together, pin G to K, starting at the neck edge, with #9 matching #9 of the I-H-K unit and #8 of G matched to #8 of panel H. Continue pinning G around to Piece I, matching #7 on I to #7 on G. Baste all parts in place. Machine stitch the doll's head front (G) to the doll's head back (I-H-K) unit. Trim the seams on the curves to within ⅛" of the seamline to facilitate turning. Turn the head unit right-side out.

Main Part of Body and Assembly

1. Take central body parts J. With right sides of material facing each other, stitch the two J parts together from #10 to #11, and continue around to #14, matching seam allowances and numbers on the two parts. Be sure to leave the stuffing opening at the top unsewn

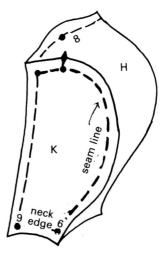

30–1 Seaming the side part (K) of the back of the doll's head to the center back of the head (H). Wrong side of material is facing out.

for now. Trim the curves to within ⅛" of seamline to ease seams.

2. Turn the main body unit right side out. Stuff the body and head units, as you did with the arms and legs. When they are full, pin and baste the head unit to the body unit, centering the head over the body. Be sure the seam allowances are tucked on the inside of the pieces, not sticking out. Overcast the head to the body with strong thread.

3. Take the arms and legs, and pin them to the body unit so that the button placement mark on J is directly under the button placement mark on each arm or leg. Each arm and leg is attached by hand stitching that goes through a button, through the arm (or leg), and then through the body. Use strong thread and a needle for the stitching. Push the needle through the button, limb, and body to the back of the body, make a small stitch, and pass the needle again through the body, the arm, and the button, as you would to sew on a button. Repeat the stitching several times to strengthen the joint. The button functions as a swivel joint. The top of the shoulder of each arm and the top of the thigh of each leg is free to rotate.

No face! No hair! Don't you love this doll?

Apron Construction

1. Actually this apron is rather like a smock. Take Piece D. To finish the armhole openings, roll a handkerchief-style hem (make a tight roll of about ¼" of seam allowance around a needle, slide it off, and attach it with a fine overcast stitch to the wrong side of the material, taking a stitch every ¼" or so).

2. With right sides of material facing each other, stitch the apron front to the apron back at the shoulders from #1 to #3 on the pattern, matching numbers and notches (Figure 30–2).

3. Take the neck facing you cut earlier (¾" × 8½") and turn under a ¼" hem on one of the long sides, with the ¼" going to the wrong side of the material. Stitch

hem down. Turn the apron right-side out. Pin the neck facing to the neckline of the apron so that their raw edges are matching and right sides are facing, starting at #4 of one apron back and working around to the #4 of the other apron back. Turn facing inside, pin and slip stitch in place on apron.

4. Press the ¼″ seam allowance of the back opening of the apron to the wrong side of the material and stitch it down. Attach one-half of a small snap at the top of each apron back to hold the apron together (the back remains open).

5. At the bottom of the apron, press ¼″ to the wrong side of material, then fold up ½″ to 1″ for the bottom hem. Pin in place and hand or machine stitch.

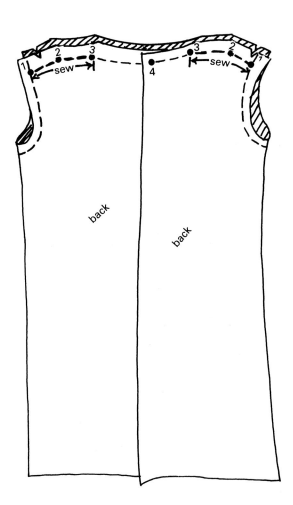

30–2   *Apron construction for Amish Doll. Seam the back of the apron to the front at the shoulders.*

Bonnet

Unless noted, construction is with right sides of material together and ¼″ seam allowances.

1. Take two L pieces (bonnet crown). With right sides of material facing, pin, baste and seam pieces together from #1 on pattern through #5, matching numbers on each piece and leaving the bottom line from #5 to #1 open. Trim curves to within ⅛″ of seamline. Turn the bonnet crown right side out and press it.

2. Cut a 9″ × 10″ piece of black broadcloth for the bonnet brim. Fold it lengthwise with right sides facing, so that it makes a 4.5″ × 10″ rectangle. Stitch across the short ends, leaving the long side open. Turn the bonnet brim right-side out and press it.

3. Take the 2⅝″ × 9″ bonnet board or an equal size of stiff cardboard.

4. Bend wire around perimeter of bonnet board. Turn ends in a flat snail shape to avoid sharp ends protruding. Whipstitch or overcast the wire to the bonnet board. Wire will completely outline the brim.

5. Slide the bonnet board into the bonnet brim you made in Step 2. Turn the open seam allowances inside and whipstitch the opening closed. Bend the bonnet board to fit the curve of the doll's head.

6. Bring the bonnet crown up and over the brim about ½″ and blindstitch it to the brim cover.

7. To make the bonnet ruffle, cut a 4½″ × 13½″ piece of black broadcloth and fold it in half lengthwise, with right sides facing, to make a 2¼″ × 13½″ rectangle. Stitch along seam lines on one long and one short side, leaving one short side open. Turn the ruffle right side out and press. Slipstitch the second short side closed, turning seam allowances inside.

8. Run a double line of basting stitches along the length of the ruffle ¼″ and ⅛″ in from the edge. Pull them gently to gather them and fit the ruffle around the neck edge of the bonnet. Handstitch it in place. You may find you must take up a little extra fullness of bonnet crown as the ruffle is attached.

9. Sew ribbons at the neck edges of the bonnet crown.

Dress your new Amish doll and imagine a winning smile on her face.

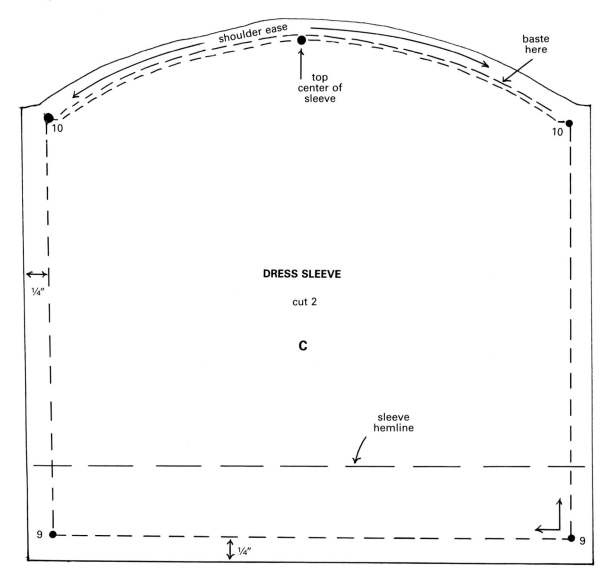

shoulder ease

baste here

top center of sleeve

10

10

¼"

DRESS SLEEVE

cut 2

C

sleeve hemline

9

9

¼"

Full-size patterns for Amish Doll's dress bodice. Dashed (inner) line is seam line. Outer line is cutting line. Arrows indicate the straight grain of fabric.

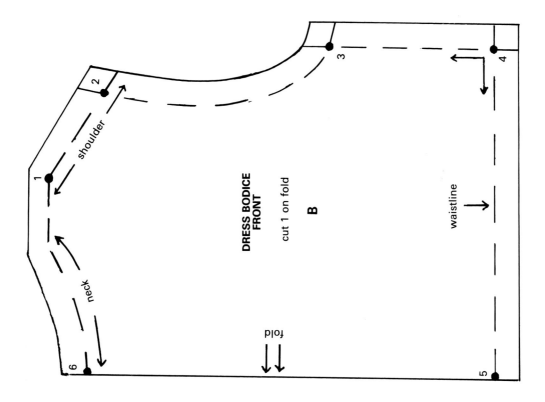

DRESS BODICE
FRONT

cut 1 on fold

B

shoulder

neck

2

1

3

4

6

5

waistline

fold

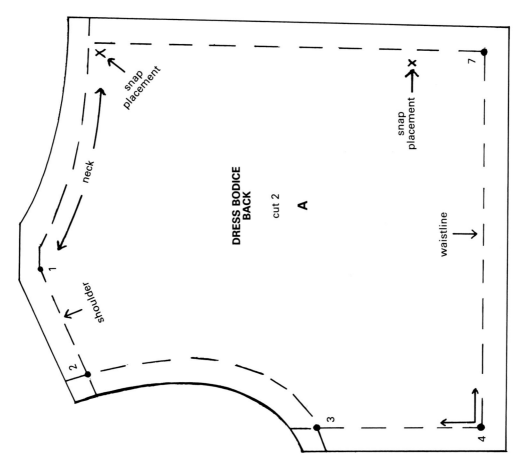

DRESS BODICE
BACK

cut 2

A

snap
placement

snap
placement

neck

shoulder

waistline

X

X

1

2

3

4

7

*Full-size doll's dress sleeve pattern. Dashed (inner) line is seam line. Outer line is cutting
line. Arrows indicate the straight grain of fabric.*

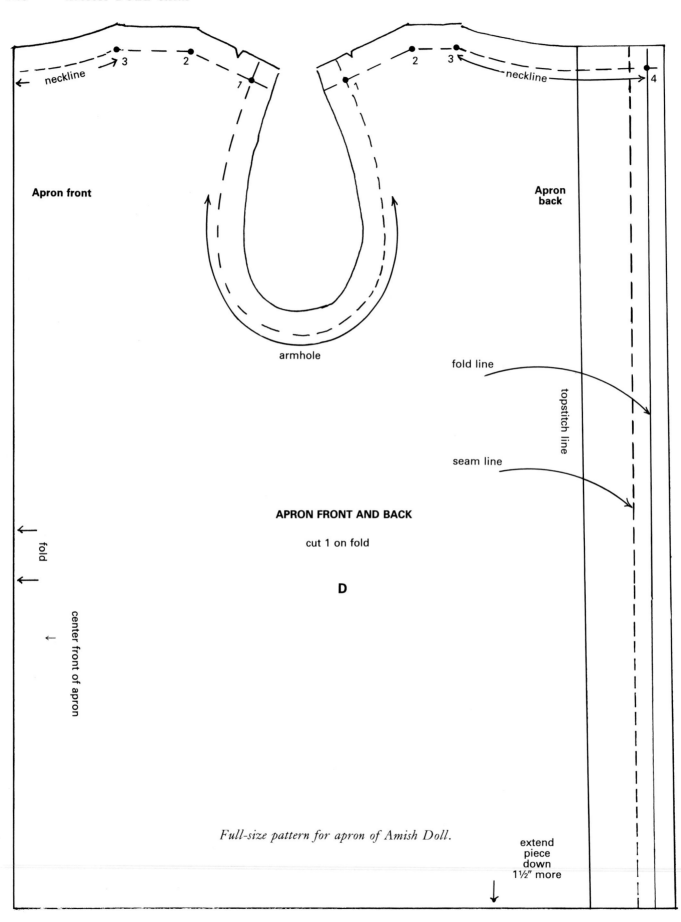

Apron front

neckline

3 2 1

armhole

Apron back

neckline

2 3 4

fold line

topstitch line

seam line

APRON FRONT AND BACK

cut 1 on fold

D

fold

center front of apron

Full-size pattern for apron of Amish Doll.

extend
piece
down
1½″ more

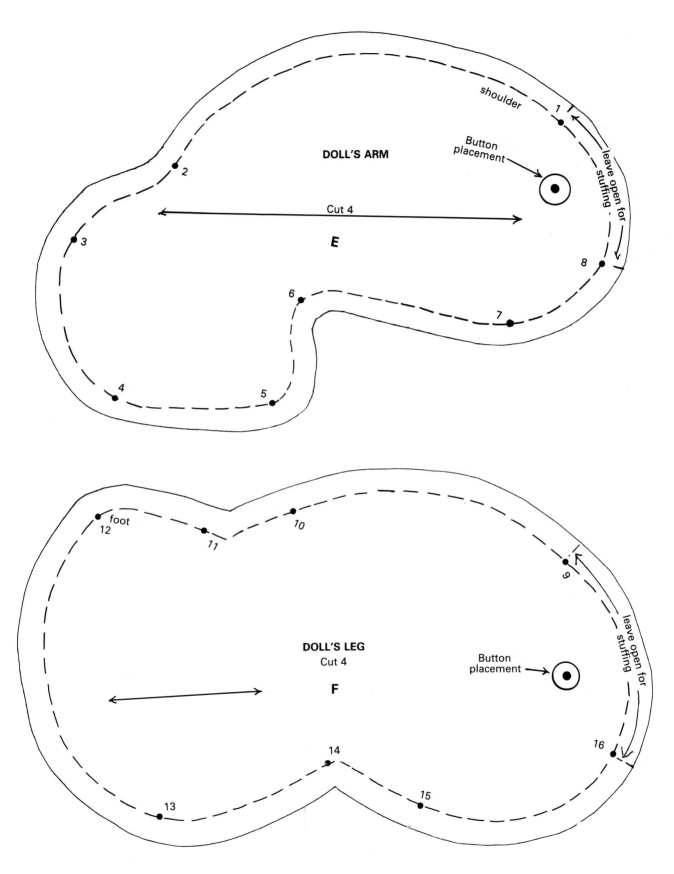

Amish Doll's arm and leg patterns, full size. Outer line is cutting line. Inner line is seam line. Arrows indicate the straight grain of fabric.

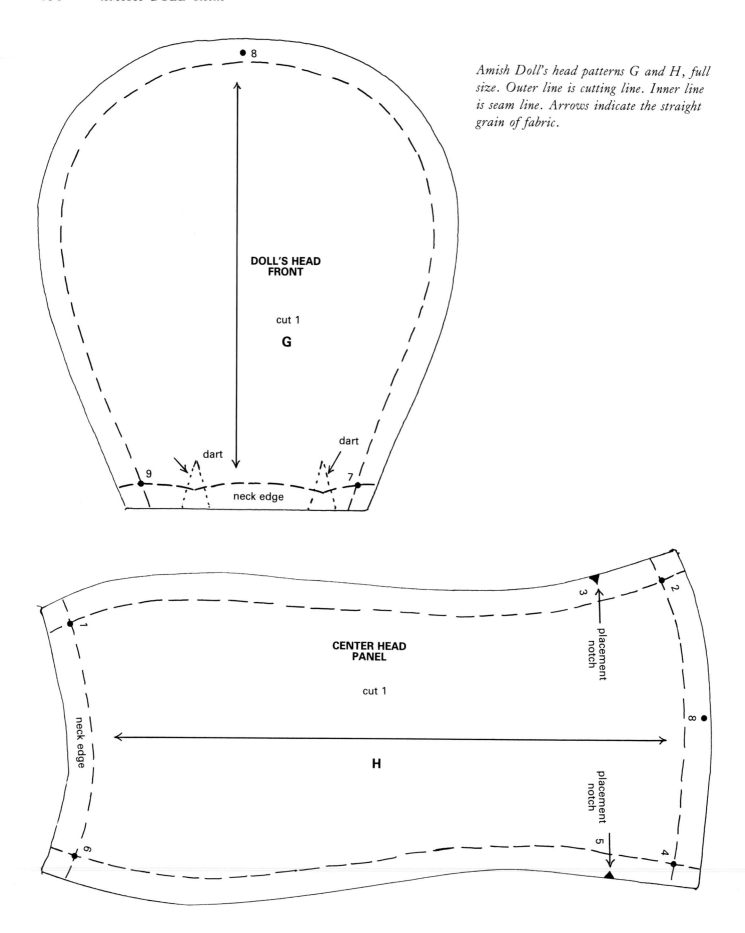

Amish Doll's head patterns G and H, full size. Outer line is cutting line. Inner line is seam line. Arrows indicate the straight grain of fabric.

DOLL'S HEAD FRONT

cut 1

G

dart   dart

neck edge

CENTER HEAD PANEL

cut 1

neck edge

H

placement notch

placement notch

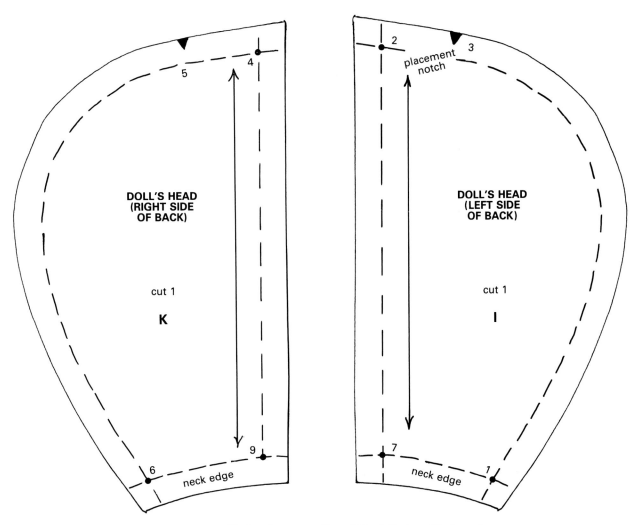

DOLL'S HEAD
(RIGHT SIDE
OF BACK)

cut 1

K

neck edge

placement
notch

DOLL'S HEAD
(LEFT SIDE
OF BACK)

cut 1

I

neck edge

*Amish Doll's head patterns I and K, full size. (Left and
right side of back of head.) Outer line is cutting line.
Inner line is seam line. Arrows indicate the straight grain
of fabric.*

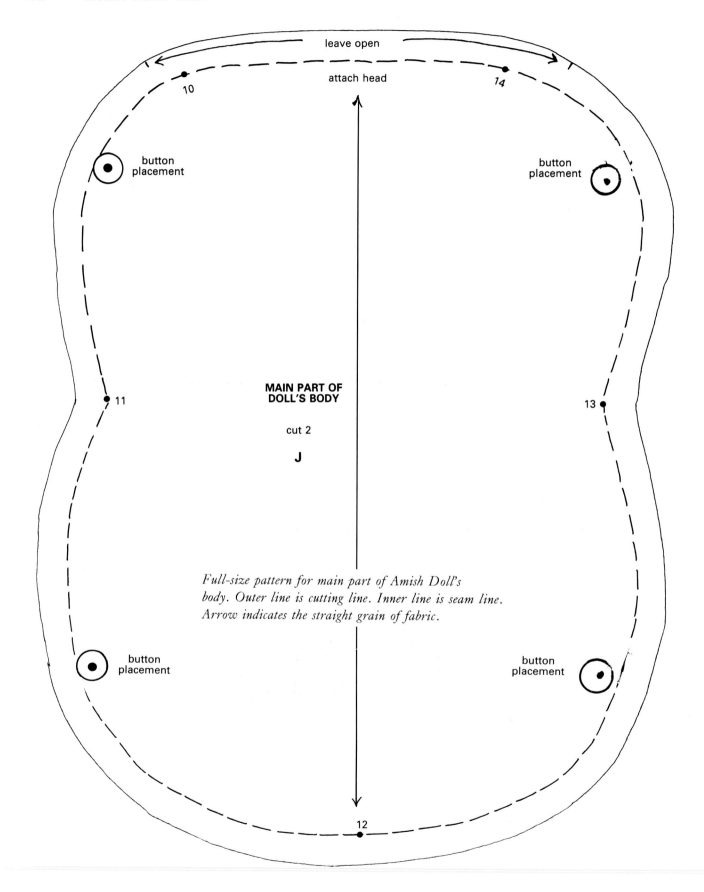

leave open

attach head

10

14

button placement

button placement

MAIN PART OF DOLL'S BODY

cut 2

J

11

13

Full-size pattern for main part of Amish Doll's body. Outer line is cutting line. Inner line is seam line. Arrow indicates the straight grain of fabric.

button placement

button placement

12

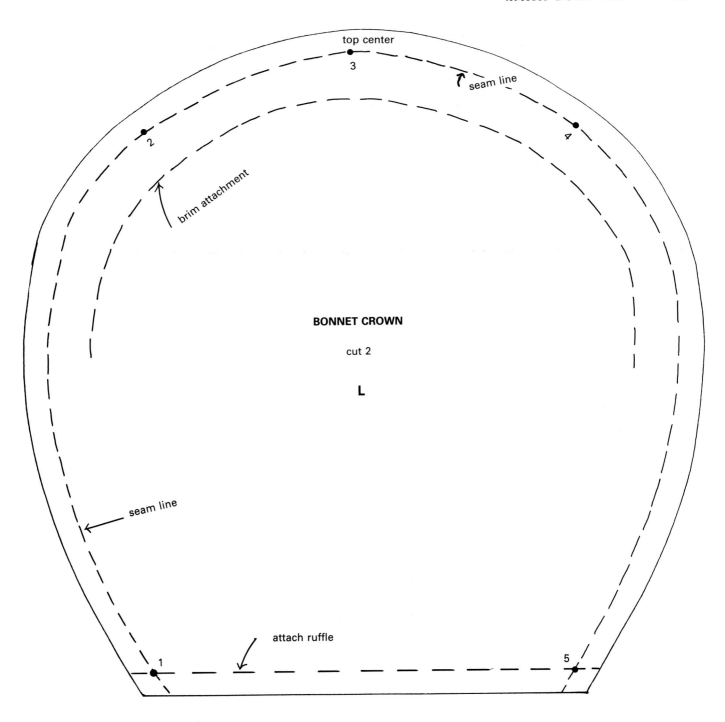

top center

3

seam line

2

brim attachment

4

BONNET CROWN

cut 2

L

seam line

attach ruffle

1

5

Amish bonnet crown, full-sized pattern. Outer line is cutting line.

A Quilting Primer

Now that we have made a quilt top—that is, we have pieced the top—it is time to quilt it. There are a number of choices to make at this point. All of them will affect the outcome of your finished quilt.

SUPPLIES

Thread

We recommend that you use what is called quilting thread. It is designed for this specific purpose and will serve you better than regular sewing thread. It is produced in a number of colors and by several manufacturers. I prefer 100% cotton thread, but I have used cotton-wrapped polyester threads with success. You may select from any of the available colors. The Amish often use black because so many dark colors, including black, appear in the piecing. There are no firm rules about color choice. If you are happy with your quilting stitches, you may select colors that contrast with the piece you are quilting. It is more likely, however, that you will prefer a color that will blend with your fabric colors. One often-used rule of thumb for Amish quilts is to match or blend with the fabric color selected for the back of your quilt. For example, if the back of your quilt is pale blue, you may select a pale blue quilting thread. It makes the back quite pleasing when the stitches blend in. If in doubt, use a neutral, off-white, khaki, or black thread.

Batting

Batting is available in cotton, cotton–polyester blend, and polyester, and in a variety of lofts or thicknesses. Which kind you select depends in part on the ultimate use of the finished quilt. Since most of the projects in this book are decorative, we recommend that you use a low-loft batting.

Needles

Quilting is done with needles called "betweens." They are short, sharp needles, which provide optimum control. The actual needle size decreases as the size number increases. A 9 is smaller than an 8. Size 12 is the smallest. Use the smallest needle you can comfortably thread and handle.

Frames

Traditionally, quilting was done on a floor frame, which occupied quite a lot of floor space. Amish quilters still do most of their quilting on floor frames. Today's homes and life-styles don't lend themselves to large frames, so a lap frame is more common today. I recommend a 14" or 18" quilting hoop. Quilting hoops are a more substantial cousin of embroidery hoops. They are sturdy and allow you to keep your work properly stretched to facilitate good quilting. Many quilters today use a frame apparatus made from PVC pipe, which is square or rectangular instead of round. Your work should not be pulled too taut. Keeping some flex in the top allows you to rock your needle.

PREPARATION

Pressing the Quilt Top

Be sure to press the quilt top carefully, eliminating any puckers or tucks. Press the top from the wrong side first and then turn the top over and press from the right side as well. Press seams closed, preferably toward the darker fabric. This is not always possible when machine piecing, but it is helpful in avoiding dark seam shadows.

The Backing (Lining)

The back of your quilt should be made of fabrics that are compatible with the top. A cotton pieced top should have a cotton back. You should prewash all fabrics selected for the back. The back of the quilt should be pressed in preparation for basting. If seams were required to make the quilt back the appropriate size, the seams should be pressed open to reduce bulk. In general, the seams joining the sections of the back will be positioned vertically—on the length, rather than on the width of the quilt.

The Batting

Take the batting out of the package and open it out flat several hours before you baste the layers together. This will relax creases caused by packaging. Cut the batting to the size given in the project instructions before basting. Batting dimensions given in the projects are several inches larger than the top.

Transferring a Quilting Design

Most Amish quilters mark the designs in the quilting frame as the quilting progresses. This may be your choice also. If so, you need a template or stencil of the design. This is placed on top of the quilt and traced. You may develop your own quilting designs, using the suggestions and instructions in the section on designing motifs further on in this chapter, or you may select from hundreds of commercially produced quilting stencils. We encourage you to try your hand at creating your own designs. They will better fit the spaces you have and will add your unique personal touch to the quilting.

If your plan is to mark all of the designs before basting, we recommend the use of a lightbox, light table, or other light source. Use only marking pencils that you have tested, ones you are sure can be removed easily or will brush away as you quilt. Nothing mars the look of a finished quilt like visible marks remaining on the quilt.

Basting

On the floor or on a protected table large enough to accommodate your entire quilt's size, spread the backing flat. Seams, if there are any in the backing, should be face up. When it is smoothed quite flat but not stretched beyond its size, anchor the backing with pins or tape. I use my carpeted floor and place T-pins all around the perimeter (edge) of the back. If you are working on a table top, protect it with a dressmaker's cutting board; it's cardboard and will allow you to put pins into it to anchor the work.

Next, gently spread the batting. Center it on the quilt back. Finally lay your quilt top down, face-up and centered on the batting and backing. Anchor all three layers to avoid their slipping while you baste. Baste through all three layers, beginning at the center of the quilt top. Use white or light-colored thread and a long, fine "sharp" needle to baste. Run a line of basting stitches from the center to the top edge and bottom edge, and to each side of the top, catching all three layers in the stitches. Each line of basting begins in the center of the quilt. Also baste from the center to each corner of the quilt top. This is much the same as used for pillows (see basting diagram in Project 10, Figure 10–5). However, since a quilt is a larger area, it will require more basting to hold all three layers in place while you quilt. In each quadrant, crisscross the space with horizontal and vertical lines of basting. For these lines of basting, begin at the center axis lines and space basting lines not more than 9 or 10 inches apart. Finally, run basting all around the outer edges of the quilt, holding all three layers together to prevent slipping and puckering. These last basting stitches will remain in place even after you have completed the quilting and removed all the rest of the basting stitches. They help insure that the edges of the quilt are secure for the binding.

QUILT STITCHERY

With the top complete, the back and batting ready, and the three layers basted together, you are ready to quilt your project! I hope you will find this step gratifying, because "It's not a quilt 'til it's quilted."

The quilting adds necessary texture and dimension to the work. The quilting stitch is a simple running stitch; that is, a straightforward stitch in and out through all three layers of the work. Begin by cutting a length of quilting thread 18 to 20 inches long. A longer thread will encourage tangling and knots. Tie a small knot in the end of thread that you just cut from the spool. Thread has a twist direction, so knotting the cut end decreases tangling. Quilting is done with a single thread.

To begin quilting, insert your needle about a half-inch from the actual starting spot and tunnel just under the top, bringing the needle up at the beginning of your line of stitching. Pull the thread taut and just snap the knot through to the inside layers of the quilt. This buries the knot in the batting layer. The closely worked small quilting stitches will anchor that knot.

To quilt, you may take one or several stitches at a time. Always try to insert the needle perpendicular to the surface of the top. Just as it passes through to the back of the quilt, tip the needle back and come back up through to the top of the quilt. You may pull this stitch through or add more stitches to the needle. Never pull the needle to the back of the quilt. With a rocking motion, continue stitching until you have several stitches collected on your needle. At first, the quilting stitch seems awkward, but you will soon develop a rhythm. Consider 5 or 6 stitches per inch, counting on top, a satisfactory beginning. As you practice, you need to strive for even stitches, and as this happens you will notice that the stitches will get smaller, eventually perhaps even as small as 10 or 11 stitches per inch, counting on top.

When you have only 3 or 4 inches of thread left on your needle, you are ready to end. You end your stitches with a tiny backstitch at the end of the stitching line. After you have taken this backstitch, run the point of the needle under the top only and come up about a half-needle length away. Pull the thread tight and snip carefully, close to the top of the quilt. Rethread your needle and continue.

---

* See quilt templates section for specific motifs.

The most important aspects of successful quilting are: an even running stitch that passes through all three layers each time; starting knots buried in the batting layer; and ending threads that are left are contained in the batting layer.

You will find many different methods of reaching this goal. Quilters constantly experiment to improve the stitch, you will too. A thimble or some other protection for your pushing finger will be important to success. Quilting needles have a sharp eye and will quickly tenderize an unprotected finger. Your opposite hand index or middle finger will serve as a fulcrum for your needle. It will be pricked by the point of the needle. I simply use a small piece of white adhesive tape to protect my finger. Happy quilting. Don't be discouraged; good quilting is 90% practice!

DESIGNING AND USING QUILTING MOTIFS

As you practice transferring designs, work on large sheets of newsprint or white shelf paper or freezer paper. Map the areas for which you are designing and develop the design, making adjustments and changes as needed. For some people, the methods will become quite comfortable and natural; if you are one of them, you can then design directly on your quilt top. For many people, this may seem too daring. Paper first is a nice way to keep a reusable record of the motifs you design. It may fill the bill on some later quilt as well.

Feathering*

To do quilting designs based on feathering, there must be a spine; the spine is the line defining the shape of the motif. It can be a straight line or a closed or open line. You can also do feathering on a circle, an oval, a heart, or a twist. At first work with a straight spine, however, for practice.

Method I: Feathering on a Straight Line

Start with a straight line centered in the space you want your design to fill. You will be using a shape that is referred to as a feather. It is a slightly asymmetric teardrop shape (see Figure Q1 in this sec-

Tracing feathers on a central spine (reduced).

tion, feather 1). On that feather you will find two little notches. The initial location of the notches is arbitrary, but they will guide placement along the spine. Begin at the base of the straight line you drew and place the feathers so that the notch on the upper curve is on the spine, and trace around the feather shape. For the next feather, slide the feather template up so that the bottom notch on the second feather just hides the top of the first feather's curve and the top notch of the second curve remains along the spine. Outline the feather shape on your material beginning at the top of the previous feather, and follow it along the spine. Using the notches as guides, continue placing the feathers along the spine until you reach the topmost end of the spine line; the final teardrop is placed on top of the feather. Turn the template over and repeat the process on the other side of the line.

Method II: Feathering on an Open Curve

As with Method I, a spine is necessary to guide the feathering. Method II is used for an open curve (see Figure Q5, right). Trace a feather template and cut it out (see Figure Q1). Initial placement of the feather is arbitrary. When you have determined the angle and tilt of the selected feather template, mark or notch the feather where it touches the spine. Outline the feather shape on your material. As you slide the feather template along the spine, reposition the template each time to keep the notches on the spine.

You will notice that the feathers will change in fullness (because they don't always overlap the same amount) as they flex around inside and outside curves of the spine.

Feathers on Curved Shapes—Corners

Since feathers make stunning border motifs, you will want to know how to feather the corners in a graceful manner. You begin by treating the corners and working out along the sides. To do that you need a line representing the imagined mitre of the corner. Beginning at the mitre line, draw a line curved to the configuration you want. You will do only half of the design and then it will be flipped over and the mirror image used to complete the corner (see Template Q2). Begin at the mitre line with either a teardrop or an oval shape. Then, using the feather as you did when you practiced on the straight spine, place feathers along the curved line, letting the base of the spine determine the position of the notches and tracing each new curve by starting from the preceding feather's back and going toward the spine. Be sure that you have completed a full design motif, one that can be repeated evenly along the border length. When marking the quilt, begin in the corner, tracing off your motif and approaching the center of the border. Any adjustments need to be made as you approach the center, as this is less likely to attract attention. On a serpentine, curved spine, you will be able to use the same-sized feathers on both sides of the curve.

Circles, Ovals and Hearts

For any closed curved design, for example, a circle, you will need two feather templates—a larger one

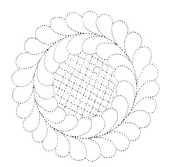

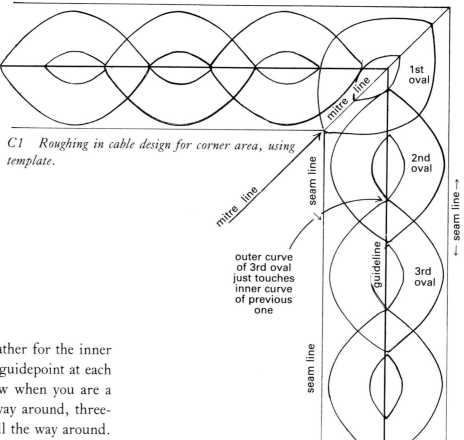

C1   *Roughing in cable design for corner area, using template.*

for the outer curve, a smaller feather for the inner curve (see Figure Q1). Mark a guidepoint at each quarter of the circle so you know when you are a quarter of the way around, halfway around, three-quarters of the way around, or all the way around.

Using the larger feather, begin by tracing the motif at one of those quarter-circle indicators. Move evenly around the curve, making a placement adjustment at each quarter-mark to absorb feathers. For example, if you have 4 feathers in one quarter circle, there should be 4 in each of the other quarters. This way you should be able to evenly distribute the feathers around the circle. On the inside of the curve, a smaller feather template is used, so that a similar number of feathers can be placed around the inside arc. Begin at a different quarter circle mark than for the outside and place the feathers, distributing and adjusting the feather placement as before. You can draw additional concentric circles (or other curves) to guide the maximum outside feather size and the maximum inside size. Be sure that all the feathers flow in the same direction on the inside and outside arcs (see Figure Q3).

Cable Designs

The single template needed for cable designs is either an oval with an interior oval cut away or a shallow S-curve. Using the oval template provided (cable design #1 of Figure Q1), draw a guideline on a piece of tracing paper that will form the center of your cable design. It is important for the cable twist to gracefully turn the corners. To assure this begin your design in the corner. Draw a line representing a corner mitre line; place the cable template so that the long axis of the first oval is directly on the mitre line (Figure C1). Trace the inside curve and the outside curve of the template. To make the second oval, turn the cable template so that its point just touches the inside of the first oval drawn for the corner. To complete the cable design along the tracing paper that runs the length of the sides of the work, continue to trace the inside and outside curves of the cable template, sliding the cable template along the guideline so the outer curve of the new oval just touches the lower edge of the inside curve of the previous oval and tracing it in that position. Working from both corners toward the center, lay out the center of the cable motif, allowing for adjustments to be made at the center of each border. Make adjustments by simply lengthening or squeezing the last two or three oval shapes as they are placed into position.

Now that you have roughly drawn the cable design on your tracing paper, you need to determine which is the upper and which is the underneath part of the cable. In order to provide the illusion of the twisting cable, one direction must always feed under the other (see Figure C2 for example). As you finalize your design, erase the outlines representing parts of the cable that pass under and connect the lines representing parts of the cable that pass over.

To create double or triple cables (see Figure Q9) you must evenly space additional lines between the original cable boundaries. You might try using your seam gauge or your compass as a calipers. By guiding the point of the compass along the already-drawn cable boundary, and using a predetermined fixed spacing, you can mark a pencil line a fixed distance away from your first cable design, thereby creating your double or triple cable.

Pumpkin Seed Borders

The pumpkin seed border is a very popular narrow border fill for Amish quilts. It provides a simple, straight design to handle narrow inside borders or lattice strips (see Figure Q11 in the quilting motifs section). To create the pumpkin seed border with a simple template, you must decide the width of the border to be marked. Cut a square from cardboard or plastic of a size such that the border width is the diagonal length of the square (Figure P1).

Beginning with the border corner and working toward the center, place the square so that its corner points touch the outer edges of the border and the inner seam line of the border (Figure P1). Keeping the square aligned with the diagonal perpendicular to the border, trace it end to end along the border. On your square template draw a line that represents the diagonal of the square and then draw two or three evenly spaced parallel guidelines on your template at regular intervals (P1, left).

C2   *Perfected cable design showing over–under illusion.*

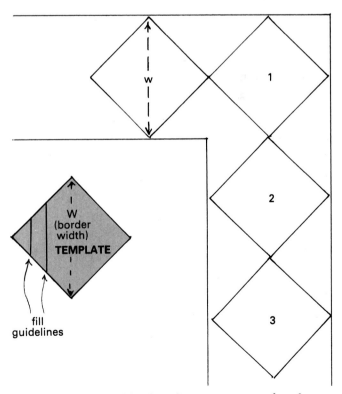

P1   *Pumpkin seed border. Cut a square template from cardboard or plastic whose diagonal measurement is equal to your border's width (w). Position and trace as shown, working from corner in.*

These lines will give the placement of the echoed squares that fill the border (see Q11 for reference). To draw the fill lines, position your square template so that its sides are parellel to the triangular shapes that were formed as the template squares you drew earlier met end to end (Figure P2). Slide the template toward the border seam until the first fill guideline on your template aligns with the border seam line. Trace the corner of the template onto the border. Then move the template so that the second guideline aligns on the border seam line; trace around the corner of the square template in its new position.

Repeat this process to fill each triangle space between the squares along the length of the border. When you have completed one side, begin the process of filling in the other side of the border. The pumpkin seed design actually takes its name from the cluster of four seed shapes in the design. Using the pattern provided (see Q11, pumpkin seed design), trace four pumpkin seeds meeting at the center point of each square. This quilting motif is rarely used on borders that are wider than three

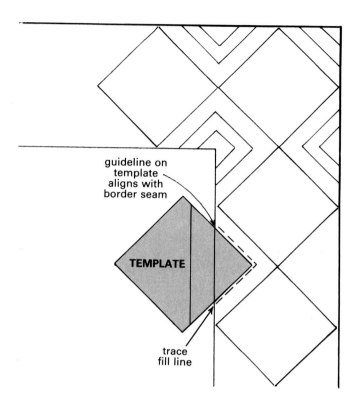

P2   For pumpkin seed border fill of triangles, position guideline on seam line and trace edges of template to make pattern.

inches. An alternate treatment at the corners is to begin so that the diagonal of the beginning square is in line with the seam joining the border to the rest of the quilt.

Teacup or Tumbler Design

The teacup design is a simple, graceful, closed design used to fill narrow borders and bars. It uses a teacup or a juice tumbler as the basic template for the motif. The key to making this design a success is that you select a circular object that has a radius (the distance from the center to the curve of the circle) greater than the width of the border or bar to be filled. While the Amish do all of their marking directly on the quilt, you will probably want to develop a design on paper before moving to the quilt.

Position your circular template so that the outer curve lies a quarter of an inch (¼") inside your seam (T1). Mark your template with a chalk line or pencil guideline, to indicate where on the

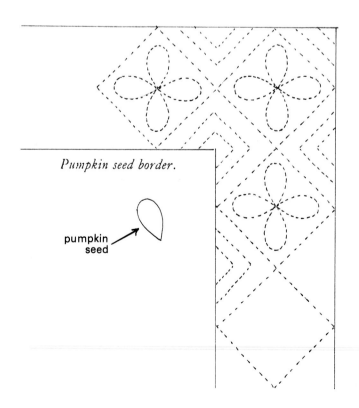

Pumpkin seed border.

pumpkin seed

circle the opposite seam occurs. This will guide placement so that your curves remain uniform. Moving along one seam line, mark around the circle with your guideline lined up on the seam line (see Figure T2). Move the template so that the new curve will begin at the end of the previous one; mark the curve, keeping the guideline lined up on the seam line. Continue marking along the entire length of the seam.

Then place the guideline on the top inner seam line with the template curve touching the outer seam. Mark the arc from A to B (Figure T3). Turn the template so that the guideline is on the right inner seam line and the edge of the template is exactly touching the outer top seam line. Mark the curve from A to D (Figure T4). Smooth the finished corner curve from B to D. It will not be an arc of a perfect circle (T5). Continue drawing the rest of the curves to complete the border design. A sample appears in the quilting motif section (Figure Q8).

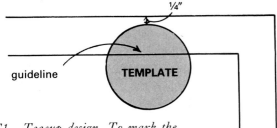

T1   Teacup design. To mark the guideline on the template, place it so that its edge is ¼" in from the border seam line. Mark the guideline on the circle where the circle crosses the opposite border seam line.

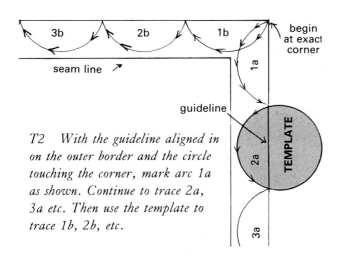

T2   With the guideline aligned in on the outer border and the circle touching the corner, mark arc 1a as shown. Continue to trace 2a, 3a etc. Then use the template to trace 1b, 2b, etc.

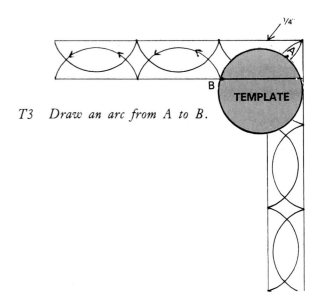

T3   Draw an arc from A to B.

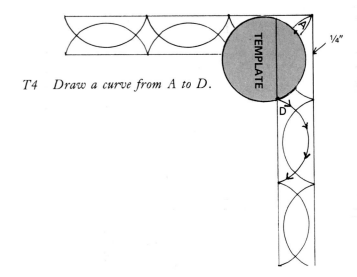

T4   Draw a curve from A to D.

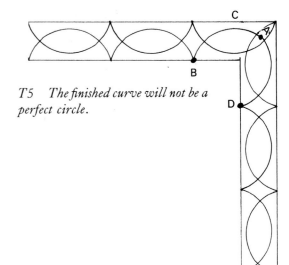

T5   The finished curve will not be a perfect circle.

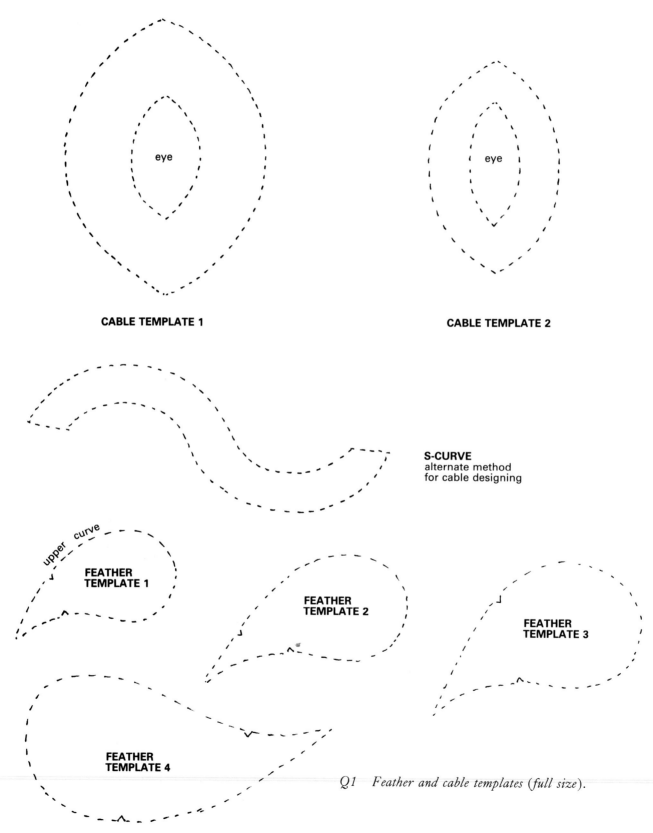

eye

CABLE TEMPLATE 1

eye

CABLE TEMPLATE 2

S-CURVE
alternate method
for cable designing

upper curve

**FEATHER
TEMPLATE 1**

**FEATHER
TEMPLATE 2**

**FEATHER
TEMPLATE 3**

**FEATHER
TEMPLATE 4**

Q1   Feather and cable templates (full size).

142

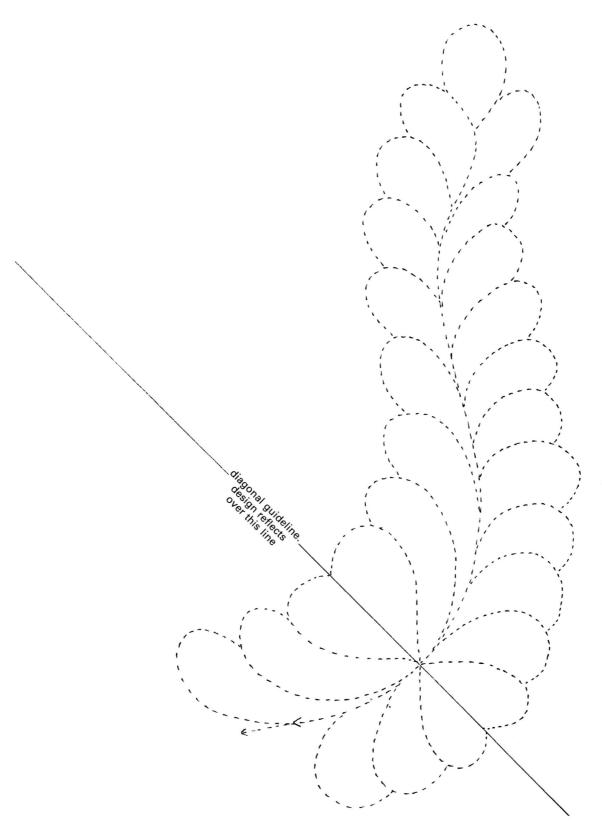

Q2   Full-size feather pattern for 36" Amish Diamond in Square. Also suitable for triangle corner area. For corners, continue the design on the left of the diagonal as a mirror image of the right side.

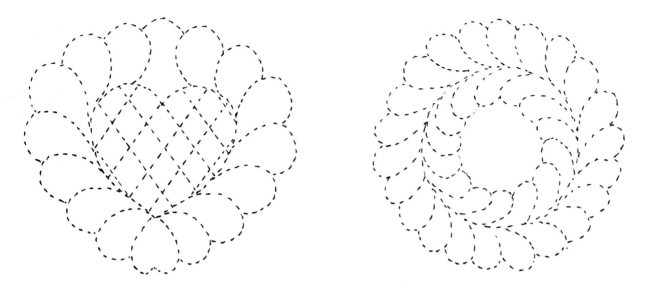

Q3   Left: Feathered heart pattern, full size. Fits 3" to 4" square. Right: Feathered circle of wreath pattern, full size. Fits 3" to 4" square.

Q4A   To make full circle, make four copies of motif Q4 and join them together with A's positioned as shown.

design center

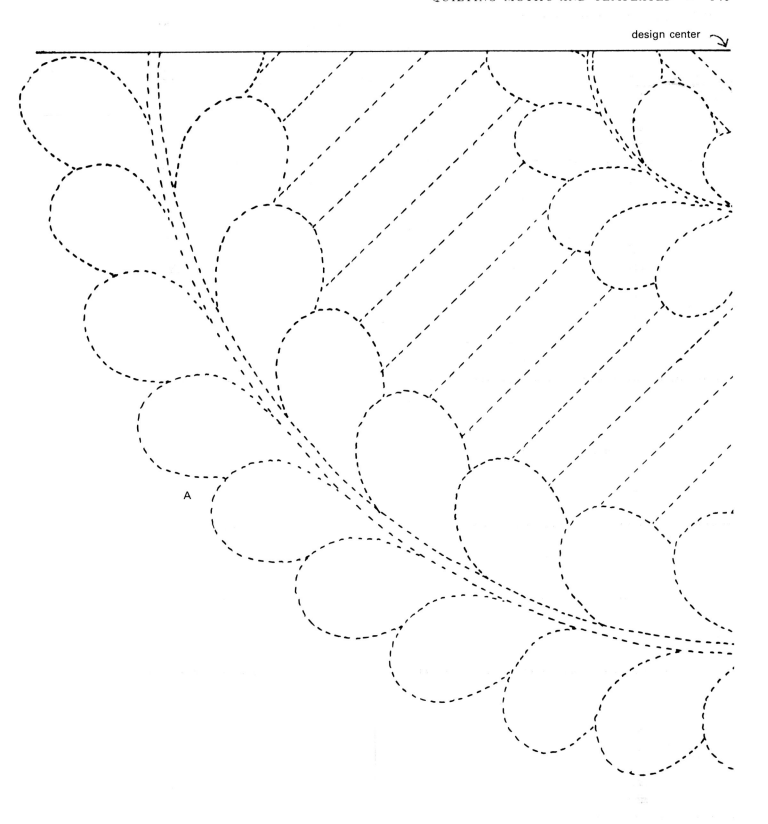

Q4   One-quarter of quilting motif (full-sized) for center square of Diamond in Square Quilt (Project 2). Background fill lines are spaced ½" apart. They should continue on the outside of the feathered circle to the seam lines also (see color photo in Project 3). To assemble quarters, see Q4A, opposite.

Q5   Left: Full-size cable motif for 2½"- to 3"-wide strip or border space. May span both borders of pillow tops.
Right: Full-sized feathered cable motif. (Feathers should be added to both sides of cable.)

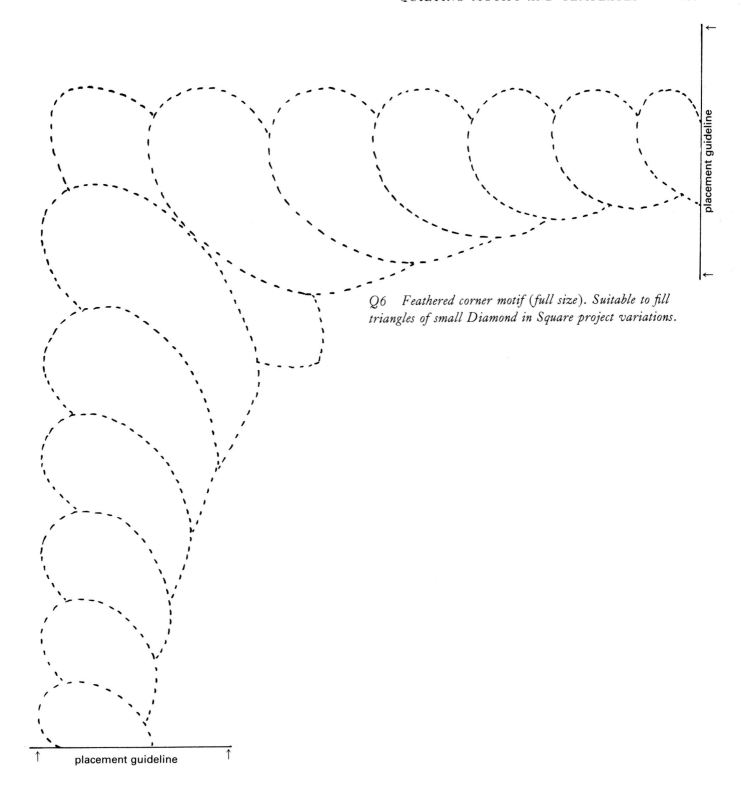

Q6 Feathered corner motif (full size). Suitable to fill triangles of small Diamond in Square project variations.

placement guideline

placement guideline

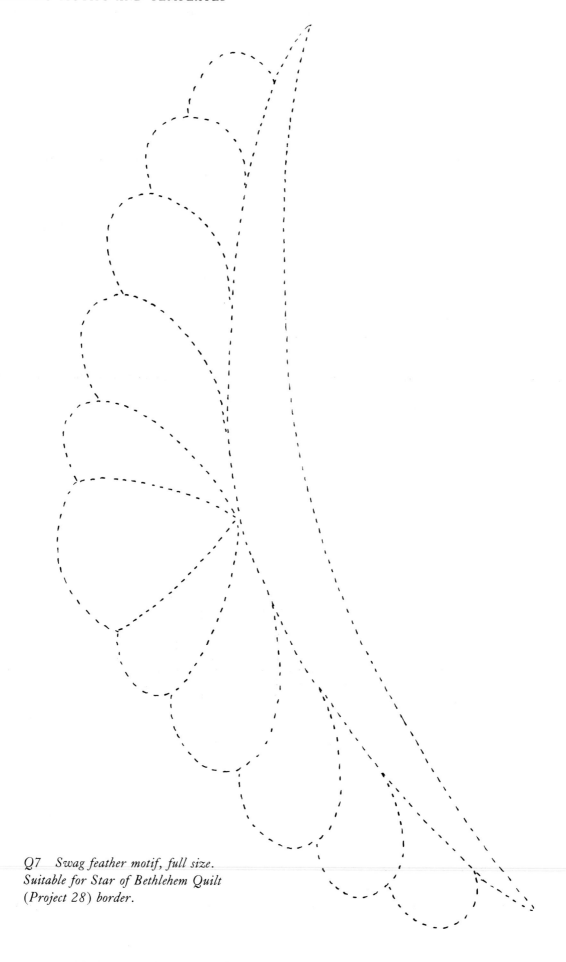

Q7 Swag feather motif, full size.
Suitable for Star of Bethlehem Quilt
(Project 28) border.

Top: Q8, teacup motif for border, full size. Bottom: Q9, double cable border design, full size. Suitable for pillow borders. The center line may be deleted to produce a single cable design.

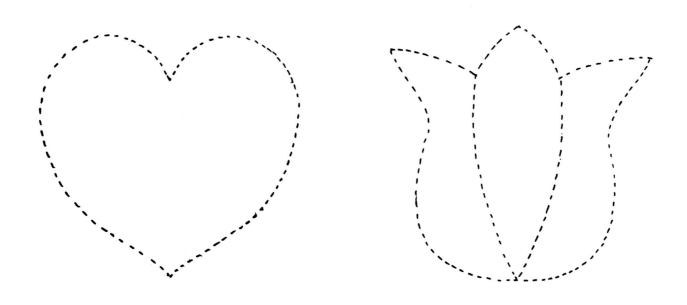

Q10   Top: Tulip circle pattern. Suitable for 3" square. Bottom: Heart motif (left) and tulip motif (right). Heart and tulip may be used for Nine-Patch Single Irish Chain Doll's Quilt (Project 27), to be placed alternately in the plain blocks.

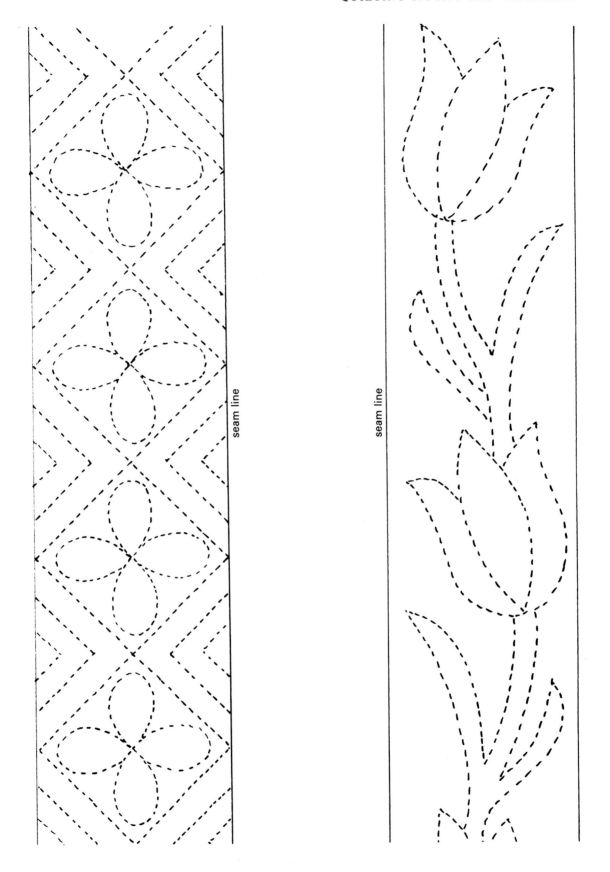

seam line

seam line

Q11 Left: Pumpkin seed border motif (full size) for 2"- wide border or strip. Right: tulip vine motif (full size) for 2"- to 3"-wide border or strip.

Q12 Top: Arc, fan, or shell motif (full size). Bottom: design that may be used for the setting squares of the Ocean Waves Quilt (Project 25).

Top left and right: Q13, grapes and grape leaf motif, suitable for Grape Basket Table Runner (Project 22). Bottom: Q14, fiddlehead quilting motif (full size). Will fit the borders of several projects.

Q15   *Full-sized feathered quilting motif designed for Double Irish Chain Quilt (Project 8).*

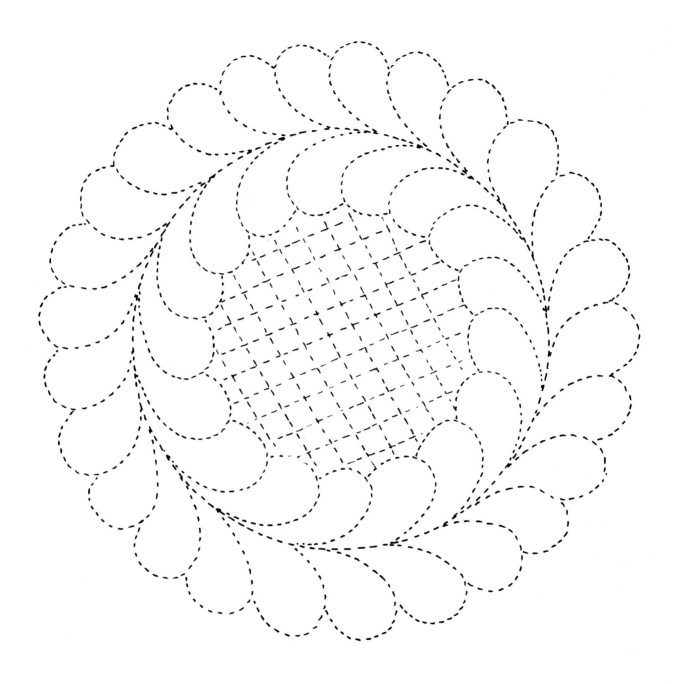

Q16   Classic feathered circle motif, with diameter of 6¼". This is suitable for unpieced squares of about 8" size. May be used on Whole Cloth Pillow center (Project 21).

Binding and Displaying Quilts

The binding on Amish quilts is most frequently cut from straight lengths of fabric or is formed by having the backing brought over the edge to form the binding. Both types are discussed below. Binding is done *after* quilting.

TYPE I BINDING: BACKING AS BINDING

A binding method of preference for Amish quilters is to use the backing (or lining) of the quilt brought around to the front to create the binding. Make the decision on how you will bind your quilt before you baste it for quilting. You *must* keep the center of your quilt top close to the center of your backing to allow adequate fabric to turn over for the binding if you plan to use the backing-as-binding method. Always complete the quilting before trimming the batting and binding.

In planning the backing, you should allow a minimum of 2″ extra on each edge before trimming the backing to size. For example, if the quilt top measures 20″ square, start with backing (or lining) and batting of 24″ square. Binding of this type is usually wider than bias binding, which can surprise you if you haven't planned ahead for it when allocating your fabric. Follow the steps given below:

1. Determine the width of the binding desired. (Remember to complete the quilting before trimming the backing or batting.)
2. Trim the batting *only* (not the backing), leaving the surrounding edge of batting beyond the size of the quilt top of the size given in column 2 of Table 1.
3. Trim the backing to the correct size, as described in column 3 of Table 1.

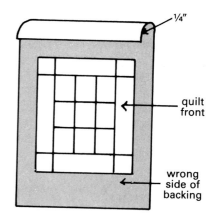

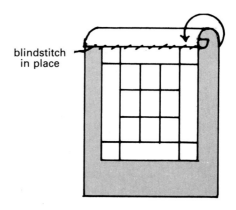

B-1 Type I Binding: backing as binding method. Top: Fold over ¼″ of back. Bottom: Fold back over front of quilt, and blindstitch it in place.

4. Fold ¼″ of material on the backing edge to the wrong side of the backing on each edge. Turn over one whole edge of backing to the front of the quilt top. Slip stitch it in place to form the

156

binding. As you complete each side of the quilt, turn and fold in the ends of each side to hide any raw or cut edges, and whipstitch the edge. *Do not mitre the corners.* Amish quiltmakers traditionally have not used mitred corners on bindings (Figure B1). This method takes a little practice, so be patient.

Table 1. Calculating the Size of the Batting and Quilt Backing for the Backing-as-Binding (Type I) Method

If Desired Binding Width (Finished and Showing) Is:	Trim Batting This Measure Larger All Around Top	Trim Backing This Measure Larger All Around Top
¼″	0″	½″
⅜″	⅛″	¾″
½″	¼″	1″
⅝″	⅜″	1¼″
¾″	½″	1½″
⅞″	⅝″	1¾″
1″	¾″	2″
1⅛″	⅞″	2¼″

TYPE II BINDING: USING FABRIC STRIPS

Bias binding is decidedly not Amish. Type II binding is a very popular alternative to bias binding that requires less fabric than bias binding does, but requires long, narrow strips.

To use Type II binding, first determine the width of finished binding you desire. Cut strips of fabric binding (see Table 2, column 3). Always cut strips 1″ longer than the finished length or width of the quilt (depending on which you are cutting). Cut 2 strips for binding the length and 2 strips for binding the width of your quilt.

1. After quilting is completed, trim the batting and backing of the quilt to the size indicated in Table 3, column 2.
2. Take the first side strip, place it on the front of the quilt with right sides of the quilt and the

Table 2. Binding Width Chart for Fabric Strip (Type II) Binding

If Desired Binding Width (Finished and Showing) Is:	Trim Batting and Backing Evenly to Exceed Top by:	Cut Binding Strip to Width of:
¼″	0″	1″
⅜″	⅛″	1¼″
½″	¼″	1½″
⅝″	⅜″	1¾″
¾″	½″	2″
⅞″	⅝″	2¼″
1″	¾″	2½″
1⅛″	⅞″	2¾″
1¼″	1″	3″
1⅜″	1⅛″	3¼″
1½″	1¼″	3½″

strip facing and long edges aligned; the strip will exceed the backing length by at least ½″ on each side.

3. Stitch strips through all four layers (strip, backing, batting, quilt top). Turn the binding strip out so that the right side of the strip faces the back of the quilt.
4. Working counterclockwise around the quilt, repeat steps 2 and 3 for the remaining three sides.
5. Turn the binding over the quilt edge to the back of the quilt; fold under ¼″ seam allowance, and slip stitch the binding to the back of the quilt. Use the extra length on each side of the strip to allow for ½″ turned under at each corner and slip stitch also. Do not mitre the corners.

Table 2 includes the widest binding appropriate to most of your quilting projects. Only a very small quilt (or wall hanging) would use ¼″ or ⅜″ binding, and it would take a larger quilt (queen- or king-sized) to need binding wider than ½″. Amish quilts often show wider bindings than "English" quilts. Be sure when you select the Type II binding method that your border quilting designs will not be covered by the binding when you turn it.

PREPARING YOUR WALL HANGINGS FOR DISPLAY

After your quilt is complete, follow the steps listed below if you wish to hang your quilt:

1. Determine which quilt edge will be at the top.
2. Cut a strip of fabric (usually the same fabric as your quilt back) 8″ wide and of length equal to the top of your wall hanging minus one inch. (For example, if the top is 43″, the strip would be 8″ × 42″.)
3. Fold the strip lengthwise and stitch it along the long side to form a tube.
4. Turn the "tube" so that the seams are on the inside.
5. Roll a hem at each end.
6. Flatten the tube so that one long side is a fold and one long side has the seam line on it.
7. Center the tube length on the quilt top center.
8. Attach the folded edge of the "tube" along the top of the quilt back, using a hand slip stitch and strong thread.
9. Smooth down and attach the long seam edge of the tube to the quilt back with a slip stitch. You now have attached the tube by both long sides, leaving the ends open.
10. Choose a dowel, café curtain rod, or flat wooden strip or stick. Make sure it is slightly longer than the quilt top. For many of the projects in this book, an old yardstick cut to size will do very well. If you wish, you may cut your dowel rod 1½″ longer than the quilt top and you may select a pair of wooden heads that fit the dowel and are decorative. The dowel, stick or rod will distribute the weight of the quilt evenly and will allow your wall hanging to hang straight and flat. Put the dowel or rod through the "tube" of material you attached on the quilt back.
11. Hang the quilt on the wall by attaching picture-frame eyelets to the dowel ends and inserting fishline, picture wire, or other suitable support to the rod ends. Or make loops of wire or line around the dowel ends. Another method of holding the rod is to rest the dowel on cup hooks or nails that are hammered into the wall at the level of the top edge of the quilt.

About the Author

Bettina Havig is a quiltmaker, teacher, former shop owner, and lecturer. She has quilted since 1970. Bettina's shop, The Quilt Cottage, in Columbia, Missouri, opened in 1977. Her interest in the Amish community dates from her discovery in the '70s that an Amish community existed only 22 miles away. Until the "Cottage" opened, her trips to the Amish community had focused on buying eggs, butter, and noodles. With the shop came a need for quilters to help complete the quilt tops that customers brought in for quilting. One contact led to another, friendships grew, and quilts were shared. The current national interest in Amish quilts has led to invitations to present lectures and workshops on Amish quilts to quilters around the country.

USEFUL TABLES

A. Metric Equivalents:
Inches to Millimetres (mm) and Centimetres (cm)

Inches	mm	cm	Inches	cm	Inches	cm
⅛	3	0.3	9	22.9	30	76.2
¼	6	0.6	10	25.4	31	78.7
⅜	10	1.0	11	27.9	32	81.3
½	13	1.3	12	30.5	33	83.8
⅝	16	1.6	13	33.0	34	86.4
¾	19	1.9	14	35.6	35	88.9
⅞	22	2.2	15	38.1	36	91.4
1	25	2.5	16	40.6	37	94.0
1¼	32	3.2	17	43.2	38	96.5
1½	38	3.8	18	45.7	39	99.1
1¾	44	4.4	19	48.3	40	101.6
2	51	5.1	20	50.8	41	104.1
2½	64	6.4	21	53.3	42	106.7
3	76	7.6	22	55.9	43	109.2
3½	89	8.9	23	58.4	44	111.8
4	102	10.2	24	61.0	45	114.3
4½	114	11.4	25	63.5	46	116.8
5	127	12.7	26	66.0	47	119.4
6	152	15.2	27	68.6	48	121.9
7	178	17.8	28	71.1	49	124.5
8	203	20.3	29	73.7	50	127.0

B. Yards Into Inches

Yards	Inches	Yards	Inches
⅛	4.5	1⅛	40.5
¼	9	1¼	45
⅜	13.5	1⅜	49.5
½	18	1½	54
⅝	22.5	1⅝	58.5
¾	27	1¾	63
⅞	31.5	1⅞	67.5
1	36	2	72

Index